A Touch of Heaven

A Touch of Heaven

A Savior's Heart

Gerald Bergeron

Order this book online at www.trafford.com
or email orders@trafford.com

Most Trafford titles are also available at major online book retailers.

Printed in Victoria, BC, Canada.

ISBN: 978-1-4269-2700-3 (sc)
ISBN: 978-1-4269-2701-0 (dj)

Library of Congress Control Number: 2010901598

*Our mission is to efficiently provide the world's finest, most comprehensive
book publishing service, enabling every author to experience success.
To find out how to publish your book, your way, and have it available
worldwide, visit us online at www.trafford.com*

Trafford rev. 04/14/2010

Trafford PUBLISHING® www.trafford.com

North America & international
toll-free: 1 888 232 4444 (USA & Canada)
phone: 250 383 6864 ♦ fax: 812 355 4082

Dedication

I would like to thank my family for encouraging me to write this boo
would like to dedicate this book to my wonderful Lord and Savior Je
who has been and always will be the greatest joy in my life. With
Him I would have nothing that is worth writing. Therefore, I take g
pleasure in dedicating this book to You my Father, to Jesus Your S
and to your wonderful Holy Spirit.

CONTENTS

Every poem is an expression, of what one holds in their heart.

Forward

Gerald Bergeron is one of the humblest and sincerest men I know. The book of poems you hold in your hand is the outpouring of that humble heart, filled with love for Jesus. Whether he's describing his own experiences, sharing his insights or relating a story from Scripture, Jerry's love for his Savior and for people shines through. His strong desire is for everyone to come into a personal relationship with God through His Son, Jesus – and that comes through as well. May you be encouraged, strengthened and drawn close to His side as you read. If that happens, Jerry will be glad!

Rev. Lonnie D. Shields
Senior Leader – New Life Christian Fellowship

Rev. Lonnie Shields

Preface

This book was written with great care to give the reader the message that God has placed within my heart. Over the years, I have written many poems and I believe each one was placed into my heart by the Holy Spirit, so that maybe someone would receive their touch of heaven. I know because I have been blessed just to have Jesus as my wonderful Lord and Savior. My prayer is that after you read these poems you will have a true desire to come to know the Savior too. Salvation was given for every person but it is received by faith. God loves you so very much and wants to spend eternity with you. That is what this book is all about my love for my Savior and His love for you. Please call on Him today and receive your touch of heaven, then you too will have a heart filled with joy. Jesus is alive and He is coming back soon. Will you be ready to meet Him in the air? If you are not absolutely sure then call on Him to save you today and your touch of heaven will be forever. God bless, and I hope to see you on the other side in eternity.

Acknowledgements:

I would like to give a special thanks to my son Ernesto Hernandez and my sister in law Gloria Barrientos for their commitment, editing skills and their share in making this book possible. I would like to thank Gerald and Lori Hernandez my son and daughter in law, for the work they placed into this book. I would like to thank James and Colleen Hernandez my son and daughter in law and Ysidra, my daughter, for choosing a great cover design. I would like to thank Don and Joni Rydbeck for their proof reading skills, and to all who lent their skills for this book. Thank you and God bless. In addition, I would like to give a special thanks to Pastor Lonnie Shields and his wife Diane for their commitment to the Lord Jesus and their love for the lost. Thank you for being faithful servants to the call on your lives. God Bless

I Am Called

I am called to take His gospel to the world far and wide. I am called to be a light that even darkness cannot hide. I am called to be the salt that adds the flavor of the Lord. I am called to carry jewels that no devil could afford. I am called to heal the broken hearted and open blinded eyes. I am called to cast out demons and expose their evil lies. I am called to take His vision and carry it to all. I am called to help the poor and hurting each time I see them fall. Then one day when I finish His calling and all my work is done. God will call me home to heaven to stand before His Son. I will fall on my knees at Jesus' feet and worship my Lord and King. Tears will begin to fill my eyes as I thank Him for everything. Then I will hear one special calling but this one will not be the same for this will be the word of God calling out my name.

Freedoms Road

One day I came to the end of the road and in sin, I felt so lost. I had nowhere left to turn and run I stood facing a rugged cross. Even though this life had still a lot to offer, the emptiness I felt inside now drew me to that rugged cross, where now I could not hide. With this entire world laid out before me, the time now came to choose. Would I now accept this sacrifice or decide again to lose? While thinking about my destiny, I wondered about that light. Would I ever come to this cross again, or would it finally fade from sight? All these things were going through my mind, but I knew it from the start. Now I had to make the choice, He was knocking at my heart. I looked back at the fun I had, as a child these ways seemed right. Yet as I faced that rugged cross, His truth came shining bright. Tears began to fill my eyes, and I knew what had to be done. I knelt before the rugged cross, and accepted God's dear Son. All of a sudden, I felt inside, as though my life was clean. It was like all the darkness leaving; His truth could now be seen. Right then I knew that I had found life, and hell had suffered loss. For I received eternal life, at the foot of the rugged cross. The blood of Jesus washed me clean, and His joy it filled my soul. I know I made the right choice, God showed me where to go. So many times, He called my name, but I was to blind to see until He brought me to that cross, where Jesus set me free.

THE STORM IS STILL

The waters raged, the thunder crashed, and lighting flashed so bright. The wind was blowing violently, and the daylight turned into night. All who witnessed this fearful sight were paralyzed inside. Surely, death was at the door, there was no place they could hide. So they turned to the one who could help calling Lord, we parish and still You sleep. This terrible storm has threatened to sink us, and carry us into the deep. He opened His eyes in amazement, and He marveled at their fear and doubt. Here they are with the Son of God, and can still see no way out. He turned and faced the raging storm, and spoke His anointed will. All His followers stood in awe, as they heard Him say, Be Still. Then at that very moment, the nighttime turned into day. The clouds were gone, the storm was over, and the danger gone away. He turned to them and said in wonder, why are you filled with fear? Don't you know that nothing can harm you, as long as I am here? That is why we must always believe, that no matter what we go through, the storms of life will be powerless, when Jesus lives in you.

A Sight To See

I often wondered what it would be like in heaven, all the things that we would see. So I let my thoughts just carry me away, to that place I have longed to be. It's where the sky is oh so beautiful, and is always blue each day. The fragrance is one that only God could create, that would melt all your worry away. I walked down all those heavenly roads; I saw flowers and none were the same. The people I passed brought joy to my heart, for all of them knew me by name. I saw beautiful angels who were praising the Lord, messengers who were doing His will. I even saw children who were servants in heaven, when He spoke they were ever so still. It feels like His love surrounds you, and what joy to be there with the Lord. While He speaks they all listen, like they're absorbing His words which are sharper then any two edged sword. The grass is so green and the water so pure, and nowhere do you find any sin. Wherever you walk you are filled with His joy, and this happens again and again. You never see darkness only the brightest of light, that illuminates straight from His throne. No one is sad or hurt anywhere, for His presence never leaves them alone. I saw many great mansions that were lining the roads; they were so bright and so beautiful too. The streets were so shiny it was like walking on gold, with its brightness reflecting off you. Animals were playing, children were laughing, and people were having a ball. There was no one in want or had a need for a thing, for God has given it all. It is kind of like earth except for the splendor and everything there always looks new. Before you ask for whatever you want, the Savior He gives it to you. Oh, heaven will be such a glorious sight, that no human could describe such a place. It is far beyond our mortal minds, and not limited to outer space. Now that I have taken a walk in my mind, to the place that the bible says will be. I wait for the day when He calls us to Him, and then He will allow us to see. The beauty and splendor I could never explain, a place that my eyes have never seen. A world so great and so wonderfully created a place that is holy and clean. One day soon we will finally stop dreaming, and wondering how heaven will be. For there up in heaven I see a door slowly opening, I see Jesus and He is coming for me.

A Servant's Heart

There was a peace that filled the room, and the fragrance was so sweet. Twelve disciples were seated in wonder, as Jesus washed their feet. One would say in scornful pride, my Lord this must not be. Jesus said, if I do not wash them, you will have no part with Me. Then when He finished this servant's lesson, He said, likewise do the same. For you must learn to be a servant, while walking in My name. For if, you wish to be the greatest, in My kingdom up above, then you must have a servant's heart, serving with God's love. Your service is the greatest work; you can give to those you see. Then as they see the love of the Father, they will know you have been with Me. I promise I will not leave you helpless, in your service to the lost. For I will give you all you will need, no matter what the cost. All I ask is that you obey My words, and always let your love be true. Then the world will know that you are different, they will see that I live in you.

FEED MY SHEEP

I turned to face the Savior, His glimpse it caught my eye. Oh, Lord I could never deny You that is impossible I would rather die. But at that very moment when my words began to part, the rooster crowed and He looked at me, His stare it broke my heart. I fled that place in agony; did I really deny my Lord? Did my words betray His trust in me; it sliced me like a sword. As I stood there weeping I could see no hope, and it hurt from deep within. For down inside my pitiful soul, I cried please forgive my sin. The days went by and the hurting stayed, could I ever face my King? Then as I came to the empty tomb, my spirit began to sing. The Lord had promised He would return, and I prayed He would forgive my past. My mourning then was turned to joy, when I saw the Lord at last. He said do you love Me Simon, and my tears began to fall. I said Lord you know I love You, my Lord You know it all. Then as Jesus finished speaking, I turned and saw Him smile. Right then I knew He had forgiven me, even though I failed my trial. Then He said I love you, now go, and feed My sheep. I felt His love inside my soul, a feeling that was so sweet. Then the Lord breathed on all of us, and we knew it would be all right. We watched as He was lifted up, and taken from our sight. We understood what He was telling us, that one day we would join Him too. So always, remember that no one is perfect, for Peter just could have been you.

A Place Called Calvary

There is a path that leads to heaven, a narrow road indeed. Every soul who finds this way, discover they are freed. There is another path, which leads to destruction, and many will go this way. But when they reach the gates of hell, they will find they have to stay. The narrow leads to heaven, where only the righteous will get in. Those who have called on Jesus, to wash away their sin. The wide one leads to unspeakable suffering, where the fire will never go out. Those who are on this deadly road have lived their lives in doubt. Two different paths that take a sinner, to their choice in eternity. One will lock them into eternal torment; the other will set them free. The wide road is one that many will find; it is disguised as pleasure untold. Yet you find it was deceiving, as you reach the end of this road. Still all who have chosen the narrow road are met with peace and love. For waiting for them at the end of this road, is the God of heaven above. And on the narrow road if you stop and look back, you will discover just why you are free. For this road will start at a rugged cross, and a place called Calvary.

I Finished The Race

I am running in a special race, I run to obtain the prize. I may stumble and fall along the way, but this should come as no surprise. That devil is hiding down many of those roads; he is trying to block my way. But Jesus is always cheering me on, increasing my faith everyday. I never grow weary while running this race, for my reward will be ever so grand. Then when I arrive at the end of my day, my Lord will take hold of my hand. He will say welcome good and faithful servant, now enter My Father's rest. For you have finished the course and kept the faith, and done your very best. I know there have been many obstacles, which have made you slow a bit. But you ran as though you would obtain the prize, and you never gave up or quit. So now, you will wear the crown of life, and your racing days will be through. You are a member of this royal family, and My child I will always love you. All that I have is yours to enjoy, with no sorrow or no more sin. Now you can live with Me here in heaven, and never have to worry again. You have finished the race as a champion; you kept the faith in stride. Every time you called My name, I was right there by your side.

Faith In The Fire

I am going to give you one more chance, to deny this one you call Lord. These were the words of an evil tyrant, who threatened them with his sword. They kept the faith and trusted God, even knowing that they would die. One by one, they chose to lay down their lives, never stopping to ask, God why. Some were thrown to the lions, while others were ran thru with the spear. Yet in their darkest moments, they believed that God was near. They were burned at the stake while their children watched all these horrors they would have to see. Told to reject the Son of God, if they wanted to go free. Yet nothing would break their solid faith, nothing could make them fold. For they were given a sure foundation, far richer then silver or gold. Their sights were set on a heavenly city, the place they have longed to be. Where God would always watch over them, and Jesus they would see. No whippings, rods, or crucifixions could make them lose their way. They knew in death they would live again, to be with Jesus that very day. It angered those who did not believe, even kings who were born to rule. They said; what is the matter with these stubborn people, what makes them act like a fool. Yet as they came to their moment of truth, they would gladly accept their fate. Even when they were tormented or beaten, their enemy they refused to hate. As the flames encircled their bodies, their eyes would close at last. Then all their pain and torment was over, forever in their past. There awaiting these precious saints, was Jesus to welcome each one. Tears of joy began flowing in heaven, as they heard Him say, well done.

At One Ment

The blood stained cross on Calvary's hill, a reminder that the debt was paid. All the sins past, present, and future, the payment has been made. When Jesus said it is finished, and the sacrifice was done. All the guilt and all the punishment were placed upon God's Son. The earth turned dark and violently shook, while evil dropped the reigns. Cleansing blood dripped to the earth, flowing from Emmanuel's veins. The Father watched from heaven, as they viciously attacked His Son. His wrath held back by a loving heart, so atonement could be won. The carnal side of the Son of God now breathed His final breath. Committing His spirit to His Father above, He closed His eyes in death. Hell and all its minions were waiting for victory to arrive. Yet three days later, they just stood in awe, to see that Jesus was alive. He took the keys of death and hell, and removed its mortal sting. Then He stepped back into His body again, as Savior, Lord, and King. Now He is alive forever more, to remove every person's sin. One day He will mount His horse, and the Lord will come again. The sacrifice for atonement required a lamb to die. Jesus became that sacrifice that the world would crucify. We are saved from the entire penalty, and our redemption has been made. For the Lamb of God laid down His life, and stamped our judgment paid.

My Wife My Love

My love you are someone I care about, and I have loved you from the start. You may never know how much I care, what I have hidden in my heart. If I were to live this life again, I would want you there by my side. For without you my life would be empty, and the pain would be hard to hide. In this life, I could not give you everything, but my love I sure have tried. When I have seen you, go without, the tears I have kept inside. We made it through some real hard times, and God met each and every need. Many times, we have gone without, so our children we could feed. It is hard to tell you just how I feel, but my love for you is strong. We have lived a wonderful life together, and we are right where we belong. So I know we will go on loving each other, until that final day. When God decides to call us home and our lives do pass away. My love if I am taken from you, there is one thing you should know. I will be waiting for you in heaven, because I love you so.

Gerald and wife Betty at new life Christian fellowship church.

GOD'S PUZZLE

The bible is like a puzzle, each piece contains a plan. With the sixty-six pieces in this puzzle, the outcome is so grand. There were many authors who added their pieces, inspired to write God's design. For it was God who gave them the pieces, so that each one would fall in line. Not even one piece could be missing, or His plan could not be complete. But they beautifully came together, and the plan was oh so sweet. Still men kept trying to change the pieces, to the way they wanted them to fit. It made the pieces harder to see, so the plan they could not get. They cut away the good stuff, and they added of their own. They could not see where God had warned them, to leave His plan alone. Darkness quickly filled the place, and the design they could not view. The puzzle God had given them, they replaced with something new. But God still kept His plan intact, His puzzle still complete. Those who were now His enemy's would be crushed beneath His feet. While all who took His plan to heart, and accepted His gift of grace. Could gaze upon His wonderful puzzle, and clearly see His face. It started with the fall of man, and every puzzle piece now would cost. When He put the final piece in place, His plan would save the lost. For there in this picture laid out in His puzzle, a cross came into sight. There on that cross was the Son of God, and the puzzle filled with light. Then as you looked more closely, the pieces changed again. A stream of blood flowed from the Lord, to wash away all sin. Many people have viewed this puzzle, to try to see His plan. But they missed the most important piece, which was at the Father's right hand. One day that piece will be returned, and the puzzle will be so sweet. Then the world will finally see the truth, for God's plan will be complete.

Nana's Chair

She would stay up reading her bible, into the early morning light. Then start each new day praying, that her children would be safe that night. She would lift their names before the Lord, and pray for their salvation too. They would hear her praying often, for this she would always do. Well nana has gotten older, and the years have taken its toll. But no matter if, nana could barely see, to God's word she would always go. Time has gone by and she has passed away, but her bible still sits by her chair. Even though her children are grown and married, her memory still lingers there. Many children were lifted to God, by nana's that trusted his word. They would pray for those that they loved so much, never quitting until their prayers were heard. These prayer warriors would stay in the shadows, many sleepless nights untold. Just lifting their loved ones up to God, a treasure more costly then gold. Now they leave their legacy, all these champion's of the Lord. They have lifted their voices to heavens shore, as they carried God's eternal sword. Still somewhere in their family, another one takes their place. Someone who was brought before the Lord, to received His saving grace. They will pray for all their children, while placing them in God's care. Praying into the early morning, sitting in nanas chair. Thinking back to many years ago, when God's Spirit kept nana strong. Where her faith was seen in every trial, and practiced all week long. Though nana is now with Jesus, her faith is always there. For every one who remembers nana, see's the bible by her chair. Please pray for your children's children, and lift them to the Lord. Always remember to read God's word, that all eternal sword. Pray for their salvation, while lifting each name with care. Then one day you may be the one, to sit in nanas chair.

Nana Ysidra Rodriguez setting on porch at family gathering.

Sweet Anointing

I like to feel that oil of joy, which God pours out on me. His wonderful sweet anointing, that he gives so graciously. The precious Holy Spirit, my helper and my friend. The One who leads me to all truth, until the very end. A stream of joy that floods my soul, and causes doubt to flee. The Spirit of my Lord and Savior, who lives inside of me. In His peace, I find a place, where He and I often meet. There He fills me with His joy, and makes my life complete. Help me Lord to serve with faith, and refresh me in each spiritual fight. So that I can stand against the enemy, in Your power and Your might. Let Your sweet anointing flow, where I lose myself in You. Place me where You want me Lord, then I will know what I have to do. Then if I happen to win a crown, my joy will be so sweet. For as I bow before Your throne, I will lay it at Your feet. Until You come for me my Lord, in Your presence I will always be. Knowing I am filled with Your wonderful Spirit, with Your sweet anointing on me.

Daddy's Little Girl

My God has truly blessed me, more then you will know. For He gave me a precious gift from heaven, and allowed me to watch her grow. We prayed for a perfect baby girl that would be beautiful in every way. God reached down and blessed us, and what a wonderful blessing He made. When she was just a baby, I would carry her in my arm. I would sing to her, as I did for my boys, and keep her from all harm. I would watch my little girl Ysidra grow, thanking God for her each day. We would cover her in the blood of Jesus, every time that we would pray. God has blessed our family, with a gift like a priceless pearl. For from His heart He gave to us, a very precious girl. He made our baby beautiful, with a heart that is filled with love. He placed in her a Christian spirit, born from God above. I am the greatest dad on earth, who God has allowed to see. That He gave a gift so wonderfully made, and this gift He gave to me. Sometimes I cry from deep within, for I am the happiest man you will know. Because He gave us our wonderful children, and blest this family so. One day we will all be in heaven, when we take that heavenly ride. Standing there on streets of gold, my family will be by my side.

Ysidra Bergeron at age of 13 taken in 2009
truly our blessing from the Father.

THE INNOCENT

I used to walk in darkness, where life meant nothing to me. I was chained to fear and hopelessness, and nothing could set me free. I was wandering aimlessly through this world, waiting to meet my fate. Not knowing what would be ahead, always first yet always late. Then one day in my darkened room, a light began to shine. All my fear and hopelessness left, and I felt that I would be fine. The very corners of the darkness began to fill with light. Right then I knew that something was different, and that I would be all right. There in that light I saw a Lamb, so beautiful and yet so frail. I saw my sins and all my faults, and all the times that I would fail. Then as I glanced back to that Lamb, I watched as He was slain. I spotted a robe as white as snow, in the place where my sins were laying. Yet as I reached to take the robe, my heart was at a loss. For I saw that Lamb being crucified, He was nailed to a wooden cross. Then I finally realized why the innocent had to die. I hung my head in bitter shame, and then I began to cry. All because I had no hope, and I could not see His love. Yet God looked down on my broken spirit, and felt my pain above. He shined that light into my world, and there restored my loss. He paid the price for another sinner, there on that rugged cross. Every once and awhile, I gaze again, to that place where I used to be. Where His brilliant light, removed the darkness and Jesus set me free.

Day Of The Lord

The clouds disappeared and the sky rolled back, what a fearful and awesome sight. There upon a snow-white steed, was Jesus in a brilliant light. He had eyes like a flame, and a voice like thunder, and all the armies of heaven at His side. Here was the Judge who now rendered them guilty, not the Lamb that they crucified. Out of His mouth came a double-edged sword, as He spoke every word sliced the sky. He had King of Kings, and Lord of Lord's, written upon His thigh. The enemy pointed his defiant finger, with blasphemous words on his breath. While one by one, his weak little forces were all being put to death. Every word from the Lord had great power, and thousands began to fall. As their blood began to fill up the valley, the birds came to devour them all. Then in the ranks of the enemy camp, a warning came down to retreat. For all who came against the Son of God, were crushed beneath His feet. Their evil captain and his second in command were captured as his army fell. Then they were judged and both thrown alive, into a fiery pit of hell. The dragon, which caused this rebellion, was chained into a bottomless abyss. This was the enemy that caused all the evil, that devil that no one would miss. Then on this earth for a thousand years, God's children received blessings unknown. While thousand's and thousand's shouted, holy, holy, holy, as Jesus sat down on His throne.

Name Of Jesus

Jesus is the Messiah, the Prince of Peace and friend. He is called the Wonderful Counselor, whose kingdom will never end. He is called the Lord, the King of Kings; the Bread of Life is He. The Nazarene and Carpenter, who lives inside of me. He is the one who was called aside, the Master, the Teacher, and the Way. He is gone for now, but is coming again, He could be here any day. The El Shaddai, the Son of Man, and the Lamb who is called God's Son. This is the one who made the earth He created everyone. He is called the Lion of Judah; the Word of Life is He. The Cloud by Day, the Fire by Night, and the One who parted the sea. He is at the right hand of the Father, the One who intercedes. He calls the world to His saving grace, and there He meets their needs. The One who walked on water, and opened blinded eyes. Our Healer and our Savior, who saves us as He dies. He is the Kinsmen Redeemer, the water for our thirsty souls. Our Comforter when we are hurting, and our God who always knows. He is our joy when we rise in the morning, and our rest that is needed at night. He is the word that we speak when we witness, the lamp to our feet and our light. His name goes on and will never end, and is forever lifted above. Jesus the name above every name, the wonderful Savior I love. There is no other name that has the power to save, to deliver, make whole, and set free. I love to hear the name of Jesus it means everything to me.

I WILL

There beyond the Galilean shore, in the darkness of the night. Near the outskirts of this busy town, there were leapers who roamed out of site. They were hiding from those who ridiculed, and judged them to be unclean. Broken hearted and all alone, and from the world now unseen. Some would walk these dusty trails, close to the crowded square. In their hearts, they had a longing desire, wishing that they were there. Hearing the crowd sounding so alive, or maybe seeing an old friend go by. They lost all hope, being confined to death, while watching one another die. Staying in the shadows as a crowd drew near, they could scarcely hear them say. Move out of the road, and clear the paths, for Jesus is coming this way. They looked at one another, and with boldness made a dash. Knowing they were hated of all, and could face a brutal clash. Yet as they came before the Lord, expecting an angry reply. He said; do not be afraid, please come closer, you have come here now tell Me why. The crowd jumped back in horror shouting, beware they are unclean! But Jesus stepped closer and touched them, so His love for them could be seen. Lord one whispered in a broken voice, You could heal us if You will. Expecting them to throw stones in anger, and cause their blood to spill. Then He said, do not be afraid, its ok I understand. Then filled with love and compassion, He reached out to take their hand. Tears began to fill their eyes, just to feel another person's touch. Thinking how could He care about the likes of us, and why does He love us so much? Never before have they seen such mercy, for no one ever showed them this love. Truly, God has visited us, and come down from heaven above. Then Jesus said, I will, you are healed, now go show that you are clean. One fell down and worshipped Him, while the others were nowhere to be seen. Here one soul was touched by God, and would never be the same. Free to lift his head again delivered from years of shame. It does not matter how you come to Jesus, just come closer to Him, and stand still. Bring your cares and ask of Him, and hear Him say I will.

HIS BIRTH

It happened on a quiet night, as the daylight hours were worn. In a tiny wooden stable, the God of all was born. While in the heavens far above, a multitude proclaimed His birth. That the Savior born in Bethlehem would now bring peace on earth. Angels were singing in a heavenly choir, while Shepard's trembled in fear. They heard the holy proclamation, behold the Lord is here. Wise men came from distant lands, to see this marvelous sight. The long awaited Son of God was born this very night. His mother pondering all these things, her heart was filled with His love. After giving birth to the Bread of Life, a gift from heaven above. All who came to worship that night, brought their treasures to the King. They rejoiced to see God's promise fulfilled the word that made everything. Today we read the Christmas story, but do we come as they once did? Do we know the reason we celebrate, or is the real meaning hid? What will it take for you to see, the Child that Mary held dear? Do you have Him living in your heart; do you know that He is near? Take some time this Christmas day, to thank God for His Son. For it is He that brought salvation, this miracle He has done. When you bring your earthly treasure, and bow your head to pray. Tell the Lord you love Him; give your heart to Him today. Then think of the tiny baby, the Savior of all the earth. Then you will rejoice with the angels, while remembering His heavenly birth. Celebrate with all your heart, then you will understand. Why God came down to bring peace on earth, good will to every man.

My Three Sons'

God has blessed me with three wonderful sons; they all have qualities of their own. They have used these gifts to bless other people, with every seed, which they have sown. The oldest son Ernesto has a military career. We have placed him in the hands of God, trusting Jesus to always be near. Our other son is Gerald, who has qualities of his own; a wonderful father who loves his children, with faith that he has shown. Then there is James our youngest son, he loves his family too, he is always ready to lend a hand, and always there for you. My son's are blest upon this earth, and it is not because of what they can afford. It is because they have given their lives to Jesus, and all of them love the Lord. I count on them to keep the faith, to guide their families along the way. So that all of us will live in heaven, when Jesus comes for us someday. I would not trade even one of my children; they are my blessings I will have you know. For I am blessed more then any man, and my quiver is always full.

Gerald hugging James and Ernesto

Ernesto, Gerald, and James.

Don't Cry For Me

When I am no longer here my friend, do not stand and weep for me.
For I was in bondage in that earthly body, now my Lord has set me
free. Just remember all our happy times, the moments we have been
through. I could not have made it through them all, if it had not have
been for you. I know you may think this is the end, and it may hurt to
say goodbye. But heaven is only a breath away, so please wipe your tears
and don't cry. If you only knew of the joy I feel, I am finally with my
King. Just try to picture me in heaven; do you hear the angels sing? So
do not weep for that body before you, it is only an empty shell. For I
am here in this wonderful place, and believe me I feel swell. I wish that
you could see the brand new body I now own. You would place that old
one in the ground, the place where it must be sown. Heaven is such a
beautiful place, as I dreamed that it would be. I cannot explain all the
glory here, you will have to wait and see. It is such a blessing here in
heaven, where you will always want to stay. So please keep your faith in
our wonderful Lord Jesus, and you too will be here someday. Then you
and I will walk by the river, where the water is crystal clear. I cannot
wait to see the look on your face, the moment you arrive here. All of
your mourning will then be over; your heart will abound with love. For
then you will see the one true God, who is here in heaven above.

WHEN I BEHOLD YOU

Jesus please forgive me, for sinning against You alone. My sins are what brought You to the cross, those wicked seeds I have sown. I confess that I am a sinner, in need of Your saving grace. So that I can live my life for You, while on earth in this wicked place. Please wash me in Your holy blood, and remove my guilt and shame. Make me clean and fit for service; seal me with Your name. Then let me walk with You my Lord, in the cool of the day. Speak Your holy word to me; I will listen to all You say. Change my heart, and fill my soul, that the entire world will see. That I have become a child of God, and You Lord live in me. Give me the power over sin, and please help me everyday. Then come and order all of my steps, let me hear each word that You say. Stay close to me my precious Lord, that I may feel Your grace. I wait the day when I will stand in Your presence, beholding You face to face.

No Problem For Him

When all of the problems I face each day, have gotten me at a loss. When I do not know what I am supposed to do, I take them to the cross. That place where Jesus said I am free, and where He has bore my pain. I lay those burdens at the feet of the Lamb, my Savior who was slain. Then every time another problem comes, even the ones I cannot bare. I kneel before the rugged cross, and then I leave them there. When my problems start to disappear, and I no longer feel alone. I leave the place at the rugged cross, and I kneel before His throne. There I am filled with His wonderful love, with no problems anywhere. For they were placed upon that cross, and Jesus left them there.

ARMOR OF GOD

I wear the helmet of salvation that my Father gives to me. It protects my mind from drifting back to the way I used to be. On my chest, I wear a breastplate of righteousness, which helps me not to sin. It keeps my heart from wickedness, and lets no evil in. I also carry the shield of faith, which blocks each dart that is thrown. It shows the devil I belong to Jesus, and he must leave me alone. I also wear the belt of truth that keeps me in God's way. I am waiting for the day when Jesus comes back; He could be here any day. My feet are shod in the gospel of peace; I keep heaven on my mind. Rejoicing in God throughout the day, and praying all the time. The sword of the Spirit is the weapon I carry, showing Jesus is my Lord. His holy word used righteously, is sharper then any two edged sword. His hedge of protection is always around me, to guard me everyday. While God teaches me to love everyone, remembering them when I pray. With all this armor, He has given us, the enemy we are able to defeat. For there is no armor for the back of us, God's army knows no retreat

THE CUP OF SUFFERING

He walked into a quiet place, and there He knelt to pray. Always connected to His Father above, a place He would always stay. Sometimes He would pray throughout the evening, in the cold and frosting night. Nothing would keep Him from His Father's love, as He remained in heavens light. Day after day, they would see Him praying, alone in this quiet place. Everyone knew He was talking to God, for glory shown upon His face. This was the place He could always be found, for this is where He loved to go. Many would watch and wait for Him, to see the miracles He would show. But on this night when He knelt to pray, His sweat dripped like blood to the ground. There was no one to comfort the Son of God, not a person could be found. The cup was ready to be poured out, but could it now pass by the Son? With tears in His eyes and love in His heart He cried; not Mine but Your will be done. Then He went to gather His friends, for His hour was soon to arrive. This would be their last time together, while the Savior was still alive. There on the cross as the sky grew dark, they listened to every word that He said. Into Thy hands, I commit My Spirit, and then the Son of God was dead. All His followers lost their hope, to see this day arrive. But as they came to the empty tomb, they knew He was alive. Then He showed them all of the mysteries, when they saw the Lord that day. He told them He would soon come back, as they watched Him lifted away. But He left them a promise of His soon return, and by faith, they would never doubt. That one day the trumpet would sound from heaven, and the Christians would be taken out.

Offering Of Me

My Lord if there was something I could give, to show You how much I care. I would lay that treasure at Your feet, and gladly leave it there. Everything I have on earth, I would surely bring to You. If it would show how much I cared, then that is what I would do. I would help the needy, bless the poor, and preach until my face was blue. Everything You ask of me, I would gladly do for You. Still I have not done this work my Lord, and at times, I am hardly there. To tired to preach, to busy to help, and acting like I do not care. My Lord I really love You, please forgive this wayward style. Help me my Lord to do things Your way, come, and sup with me awhile. Lord, I really do love You please hear this sinner pray. Come and help me to live for You, and walk with me today. My Lord I have no gifts to offer, just one treasure I hope You will see. The gift I lay down at Your feet, my Jesus it will be me.

Not Alone

All alone in this world of darkness, and no one to understand. Like being lost in a giant desert, one tiny grain of sand. Who can deliver this wretched soul, or fill this void I bare? So many times, I have searched for an answer, but one was never there. Come my friend and follow me, to a very special place. Where you can find peace, and joy everlasting, a place of forgiveness and grace. It will not cost you anything, and you will never suffer loss. It is where this world was brought back to God; and was at the rugged cross. Where all the sins were placed long ago and the curse was taken away. Where innocent blood was shed for all, and guilt was left to stay. The Savior, who hung there for all to see, would die for all mankind. Those who came with repenting hearts, His salvation they would find. There this Lamb was sacrificed God's Son hung crucified. His precious blood was poured out for all, where the hope for each sinner now died. Sin required a sacrifice, which was death to the human race. Yet God in all of His wonderful Love sent His Son to take our place. So come to the cross and be forgiven, have faith and give Jesus a try. Then you will have eternal life, and you will never have to die.

ASK AND RECEIVE

We have sung about His amazing grace. We have felt His wonderful love. We have done His work down here on earth, and we have dreamed of Heaven above. Many times, He has spoken to us, through a person or even His word. Deep inside a still small voice, agreed to what we have heard. We have prayed for those needing healing, and mourned for those who were lost. We were glad to give to the needy, and we did not mind the cost. We have learned the bible by reading it, while His Spirit explained the plan. We have marveled in the mysteries, while He has helped us to understand. We have even gone to where He has led us, at home or to a foreign land. The enemy has tried to slow us down, but in God's power, we took our stand. It is true the church has done many things, for the cause in which we believe. Yet all these things that we have done, what honor did God receive? We did not live a life free of sin, and some, have never heard His call. We were born with a nature to disobey God, and a curse that came through the fall. No one looked for a Savior, for sin became commonplace. We were not there when He created it all, or spoke to Him face to face. We did not have to suffer, where our flesh would be torn apart. We did not hang on that rugged cross that broke the Father's heart. We did not know what would lay ahead, all the sinners He would save. We did not lay our lives down for them, to endure death hell and the grave. So what exactly did we do, to think we have done our part? The answer is we believed in Jesus, and we asked Him to come into our heart. There was nothing more that had to be done for Jesus completed the task. The only thing that we had to do was to come by faith and ask. There are many things we have done for our Savior, to fulfill our Heavenly call. Yet we are saved by what Jesus has done and He has accomplished it all.

Born Again

If I could live my life again and start all over too. I would not change what I have now, just the things that I have been through. All the times when I was wrong, and the bad things I have done. I would try to live a peaceful life and give help to everyone. I would read my bible like a starving man and I would pray like never before. I would try to do what You tell me to Lord, and not be fooled any more. I would keep my sights on heaven above, and not let Your blessings pass by. I would trust You Lord even when problems come, and never ask You why. If only I could do it again, I would live my life brand new. You know my Lord, I think I will, and You said that I could too. You said if we are born again, our life would then be new. Changed by faith in the Son of God, and Your word is always true. No more sin and no more past, completely born again. All it took was to ask You to save me, and Your Spirit entered in. Lord, You died to wash us clean, and remove our life of shame. You saved us and removed all doubt, when we called upon Your name. You are fully God and fully Man who lives to intercede. All who accept Your gift of grace will discover they are freed. You have given us this new beginning, to start out fresh and new. No more will we live in doubt we will put our faith in You.

JESUS PLEASE FORGIVE

Jesus please forgive me Lord, I am asking from my heart. Come and wash away my sins, and show me where to start. Cleanse me with Your precious blood, wash and make me clean. Purify my heart and mind, of the evil I have seen. Then come and live inside of me, make my heart Your resting place. Remove the guilt and all the shame, so that I may know Your grace. I believe You are the Son of God, who died here in my stead. Then three days later, You entered Your body, and rose up from the dead. I know that You are seated in heaven, and will one day give a shout. Then I will come to be with You, of this I have no doubt. Thank you Lord for forgiving me, and washing my sins away. I know I will spend eternity in heaven, forever with You some day. You said that I am a child of God, and You gave me righteous clout. When You left my sins hanging on the cross, and threw my old life out.

DECIDING FOR CHRIST

My friend God really loves you and He knows you really well. He is aware you are a sinner, who may in up in hell. That is why He has made a way, to save you from that place. A plan was made from the very beginning, to save the human race. That is why He left the choice, completely up to you. That if you chose to suffer in hell, there would be nothing He could do. The bible is His master plan, to seek and save the lost. His gift of life eternal would be given without cost. Some believe it is way too simple, how easy it is done. He gave this gift to the entire world, who would believe in His Only Son. It starts with faith to believe His word to accept what He says is true. To ask the Lord to forgive your sins, and to come and live in you. Just tell Him you are sorry, and confess that you believe. As His Spirit comes into your heart, what a blessing you will receive. Just ask the Lord to come into your heart, and believe His word is true. Then God will add you to His Family, and come to live in you. Then if you ever feel defeated, and it seems like your alone. You can lift your voice to the Father above, for prayer is heavens phone. Do not be afraid, to tell the Lord the way you really feel. God will receive you like a little child, which is part of this wonderful deal. You will never have to worry again, of what your future may be. God will make you a new creation, and Jesus will set you free. So raise your voice and praise Him, and receive His gift of grace. Then one day when you leave this life, you will see Him face to face

Our Supply

The world is in a panic mode, because the end is drawing near. But if you are a believer in Jesus Christ, you have nothing you have to fear. The daily news is certainly bad, with our future looking grim. Yet God says He is our deliverer, so I will put my trust in Him. Many have placed their faith in money they hold their precious stock. Then when this economy begins to fail, it sends them into shock. We need to get our eyes off our problems, and lift them up above. To Where God is seated on His throne, to welcome us with love. He has said to think first of His Kingdom, and the rest He will supply. Then He will take care of all our needs, even if our well runs dry. You may even lose your job one day, and find you are out in the cold. That is when you should keep your faith stand strong and be faithful and bold. Then as this world is panicking, not knowing what to do. They will remember all of your preaching, and will surely come to you. All the fear that kept them away will leave as they draw near. They will search for you for any message, for whatever they can hear. Then God in His wonderful mercy will soften their hardened heart. Then on their knees, they will fall before Him, a place where all must start. Then their fear and all of their worries will finally be gone at last. As they call upon the Lord and Savior, He will wash away their past. He will take away the bitterness, and forgive them for their sin. They will then receive salvation, and their new life will begin. Then as they see these terrible things happening, the things the world is going through. They will turn their hearts to Jesus saying; I am glad I now have You. Never again will they have to worry, and here is the reason why. Because Christian's will not go without, God is our supply.

YOKE OF BONDAGE

Some people say they are sick of religion, they say it has caused violence and strife. But those who have a relationship with Jesus have a better way of life. Religion has its ups and downs; and it has its teaching tools. God is the Judge of what is right and wrong; but religion just deals with rules. Do not do this, or you will go to hell, if you do that, you will get the same. But the only rule God gives for salvation, is to believe in Jesus name. If you are saved and right with God, you do not go looking for sin. Yet if you have religion without Jesus, you will have that desire again. When the Holy Spirit enters you, He points you to the shame. Then as the guilt of sin appears, you know who is to blame. Following the law will never save you; it just shows that you need to be forgiven. For only by grace can any one be saved, and for Jesus you should be living. Religion is good for those who need rules, but it will never make them good. Serving Jesus, you are lead by His Spirit, and you live the way you should. It is not about being good enough for heaven, or no one would ever get in. It is being cleansed by the blood of Jesus, who will wash away your sin. Free from the law of sin and death for the entire world to see. The reason He came to die on that cross, was to save both you and me.

Only Believe

Come and see a man who spoke to me, and told me about all of my past. Could this be the chosen Messiah, who has come to us at last? For He speaks the words of wisdom, in power and authority too. Come and meet the Man of God, He is waiting there for you. Let us go to hear Him speak, and see this Holy One. Then we will know for certain, if He is the promised Son. Listen to all of the words that He speaks, and behold how He heals the sick. No man we have heard has ever spoken this way, and His miracles can be no trick. Now we no longer need your testimony, for we have seen Him on our own. We now believe He was sent by God. His salvation has been shown. Let us ask Him to stay a while, so He can tell us what we should do. He speaks the words of eternal life, and how we can receive it too. The long awaited Son of God has finally been revealed. Now all the lost and hurting souls will finally now be healed. Tell us Lord what we must do to be saved for eternity? Just lay aside your doubt and fear, and with faith believe in Me.

Always Be With Me

They heard that the Lord had finally arrived, come quickly for He calls for you. As they went, the mourners followed, to see what He would do. One said Lord if you had been here, then my brother would not have died. With tears in her eyes, she tried to be strong, but the sadness would not subside. He felt the pain she had inside, and tried to comfort her soul. Yet even though she had faith in Him, the hurting would not go. Take Me to your brother's grave and I will raise him from this sleep. Then He groaned from within His Spirit, and the Lord began to weep. When they finally arrived to the place of the dead, He said roll away the stone. Now you will see the power of God, for now it will be shown. Everyone stood there watching, and many had their doubt. All were filled with joy and wonder, when He called the dead one out. Fear and awe went through the crowd, as they witnessed this mighty deed. Here is a man who can even stop death; He is everything we will ever need. Take away his wrappings, and let this man go free. Give him something so that he can eat, and let your doubting flee. I have the power over life and death, as you have seen today. Come to Me that you may live, I will wash your sins away. Believe in Me and you will live, and see My glory too. For I have brought salvation, which I freely give to you

Holding On To Me

I often wondered why people had to die, this question I wanted to know. He said unless a seed is planted, a flower could not grow. Then I asked about this evil world, why the wicked always seem to win. He said death would be the payment, for the pleasure of their sin. I said; then Lord why must we suffer, with pain to hard to bare? He said I remember all the pain you went through; do not forget that I was there. Then why must children be abused, their shallow lives now broken. He said those who hurt My little ones, will receive what I have spoken. Then I asked one final question, Lord why can't we see Your face? He said just look out all around you, throughout the human race. There I am with those hurting families, whose loved ones are no more. You can see Me knocking at their hearts; I am standing at the door. You can also see Me waiting, for each sinner to repent. When you were in pain, I was working there, through all the servants that I have sent. I was there to fix those broken lives, of the children that are lost. Every one who has harmed My children will one day pay the cost. I am everywhere I am needed, and I come to all who call. I can come to everyone everywhere, for I am All in All. So remember I will never leave you alone, just look and you will see. The person, who receives their miracle, is holding on to Me.

Jesus Is Alive

God looked down upon the earth, to find a righteous man. He wanted to see if any were searching, or if any did understand. A world of souls would be lost forever, with a redeemer nowhere to be found. No one on earth could save them, for no sacrifice was around. Yet He had a plan so long ago, that He would pay their price. He would send to earth His only Son, as a holy Sacrifice. As the years began to fade away, many son's and daughters died. The day drew near and now was ready, for His Son to be crucified. His cleansing blood would wash this world, a flood from Calvary's hill. The Son would carry the sins of all, to do His Father's will. The sting of death, the stench of sin and the curse upon a cross. He would now bring about salvation, or the world would suffer great loss. They beat Him like a criminal, and stripped Him of His earthly right. The Son of God would submit to man, He would die this very night. No comfort and no glory, no army at His side. Beaten and bleeding, this Suffering Servant, was now hanging crucified. God looked down and watched His Son; He longed to be at His side. His Son looked up, and said It Is Finished, and then lowered His head and died. Still the Father would not let His Son see decay, and the promise would soon arrive. For out of the tomb came the cry of victory, JESUS IS ALIVE!

MERCY

The people came to the outer court, in hopes to cover their sin. Their bulls and goats were of a perfect lot, which would surely get them in. But their sin could never be removed; this only covered up their crime. It would have to be repeated often, and covered every time. They would wait outside the holy place, while the priest would inter in. He would present himself inside the holiest place, to make atonement for their sin. As he came into the Holy of Holies, before the mercy seat. He would bring the blood of the innocent, and with God, he then would meet. Every year repeatedly, this sacrifice would take place. There behind the holy veil, God would cover up their disgrace. A tabernacle made with hands, a shadow of what would come. Leading to a better covenant, which would sanctify everyone. Jesus came to offer Himself, a sacrifice for all sin. By opening the veil to everyone, so that all could enter in. All the sins that were covered over, He washed them all away. This was the perfect sacrifice, and sin could never stay. By taking the law of sin and death, and nailing them to the tree. He left them where He was crucified, at the cross of Calvary. Then He went back to the Father, with redemption for man now made. For all could reach salvation, the entire price was paid. Now we can come into the holiest place, before His mercy seat. To know we are forgiven, because our salvation is complete.

God's Tender Grace

Our Holy Father has shown His Love, by the grace He has given from up above. Let us all remember what He has done, He offered up His Only Son. When the entire world was dead to sin, He sent His Son so we could be born again. He gave His life to show the way, then rose in glory the third day. All heaven and earth exalts His name, now and forever He is still the same. So when you lift your voice to pray, call on Jesus the only way. For His truth is seen throughout the land. God's tender grace, His outstretched hand. Do you know Him as your Savior, or are you looking for another way? Well His grace is given to those who ask, so don't let it pass away. Take the gift God gives to all; it is free to every soul. He sent His Son to take your place, and make your living whole. If you want to have the assurance of heaven to one day see God's face, then call on Jesus to save your soul. He is God's tender grace.

REPENT HE MAY COME TODAY

This world as we all know it is coming to that day. When every knee will bow to the Lord, and know He is the way. Some will say that they are sorry, but He will turn His head in shame. These were the ones who refused to believe and call upon His name. The word of God was preached to them, but pride was their big gain. So when satan is thrown into the pit of hell, they to will feel his pain. They will cry from deep within them, with suffering to great to bare. It is all because they refused God's grace, as though they did not care. The time is now getting closer, and every eye will see. Only those who believe in Jesus will escape and be set free. Just remember you can still be saved, so cry out at heavens gate. For no, one knows when the Lord will come, but that lake of fire will wait.

How Will They Feel

The day you trusted Jesus, to save your dieing soul. A question was lingering in your mind, could a sinner like me be whole? How about the friends I have, what would the old crowd think? What about my happy time, could I have just one more drink? Then you started to read your Bible, hoping to find a reply. Then the devil would say that little sin is ok, so you started believing his lie. Slowly you started to go back to your old ways, where sinning did not seem so bad. As time slowly passed, you even stopped caring, and lost all the hope you once had. All of this time Jesus stood waiting, the tears in His eyes showed His hurt. So many people have broken His heart, and trampled His blood in the dirt. Many times people fall back into sin, and the world just pulls them apart. They forget that our Savior, once died on a cross, with sinners like us in His heart. Sometimes I cry when I think of the lost, how they will feel when the rapture takes place. What will they think when their loved ones are gone; will they give up their chance at His grace? What about those, who at one time did care, how will they feel at the news? That Jesus was here, but they were left behind for believing the world's views. Now you may have friends that you drink with each day, and getting high for a time may be swell. But think for a moment about where you will be, while your friends are burning in hell. The devil can lead you astray with his lie, and that is because he is such a great liar. So why would you want to spend all of eternity, with him in the lake of fire? Do not let him steal the gift that is in you; and do not wait to get right again. For Jesus could come in the blink of an eye, and you could be judged for your sin. He is waiting until the time is right, and then He will come for His own. If you are sinning when He arrives, He just may leave you alone.

48

MY APPOINTMENT

I know that I am a sinner, who has been saved by His Loving grace.
I am waiting for that glorious day, when I see my Saviors face. It may
happen when I least expect it, and may catch me by surprise. But as I
am standing in heaven with Him, tears will be in my eyes. You see I
am waiting patiently, for my Lord to call my name. To deliver me from
this hurting world and this body steeped in shame. It is I who caused
my Lord to die; my sin is what nailed Him there. Not once did He
point His finger in blame, or say it was not fair. He took the pain that
belonged to me, and He bore my guilt and shame. Then in a special
book that He had, my Savior wrote my name. Therefore, I owe my life
to Him, at a cost that was so high. That if God demanded that we pay
the price, then everyone would have to die. But we do not have to worry;
God said the gift was free. By sending Jesus to pay the penalty, for
sinners like you and me. That is why I am filled with hope, and I know
I will see His face. I will one day stand before my Lord, in an awesome
holy place. A place where tears will be no more and the pain will be in
the past. That moment I have been waiting for, is approaching very fast.
For the trump of God will sound from heaven, and I will be lifted high.
No, matter what any one thinks of me, this man is going to cry.

Rapture Ready

When I have finally left this earth, I will not look back again. I will not care for the things I own, or the places I have been. I will leave behind my money, and everything I own. For waiting for me in heaven, are the treasures I have sown. I may be leaving many things, even people that I love. But I know if they give their lives to Jesus, we will meet in heaven above. All the things we have in this life are going to pass away. Yet the things we are storing up in heaven are guaranteed to stay. Some people may decide to stick it out; they will think they are ok. But I wonder how they will feel inside, when they see us taken away. Then will come great trouble, like there has never been before. Many will want to flee this torment, but it will only bring them more. I am not telling you this to scare you, or to cause unwanted fear. But hell is about to break out on earth, and I will not be here. Jesus our Lord is coming soon, to gather Christian souls. I am watching very closely, for that hour which no one knows. Yes all my earthly treasure, I will leave to those who stay. For everything that is left behind will quickly pass away. No matter what the pleasure is, I will gladly let it be. If you are wise you will put your faith in Jesus, then you can come with me.

Maybe Today

There are wars and even rumors of war, happening throughout this earth. With nations rising against nations, like the pains before the birth. With earthquakes, shaking many places and the gospel preached in every land. Could the tribulation start today, could destruction be at hand? Jesus said; as you see these things happening, to look up, your redemption draws near. Parents and children battling each other, it sounds as though it is here. The signs may now be visible, like they never have been before. The Lord said we should always be ready; He could be standing at the door? Many will surely be surprised, with the world unaware. It will happen in the twinkle of an eye, one blink and we are there. Yes, no one knows the day or hour, but surly today it could be. That is why I am staying ready, for when my Savior comes for me. Do not be caught with a surprise on your face, or sinning on your mind. For if, this is the moment He decides to come back, what will the Savior find? Live as if He may come today, and always be ready to go. For a shout from heaven could sound like a trumpet, and then everyone will know. Maybe you think you have a lifetime to wait, but the signs all show it is near. For in a moment in the twinkle of an eye, Jesus could be here.

The Wealth

If I could have the wealth of the world, I know what I would do. I would buy each person on earth a bible, so that everyone could learn about You. Then I would make sure that the hungry are fed, and there would be shelter for those in need. I would teach them how to plant great crops, and supply to them the seed. I would stop the world from going to war, for they would have no need to fight. All the people would be given plenty, to survive both day and night. I know this is a silly dream, and it even sounds unreal. But what would happen if we all believed in God, how would that make Him feel? People would repent of all their sin, and God would heal our land. Jesus would be the Lord of their lives and they all would understand. Peace would be a way of life, and sin would be no more. The devil would be seen as that fallen angel, not able to deceive any more. Again, this is a silly dream; imagine everyone in God's light. Doing good and praising the Lord forever in His sight. Well right now, this may just seem unreal, but I have some wonderful wealth to share. When you finally get to heaven, you will find this dream is there. But the saints will not be dreaming for this place will be so real. All who call on the name of Jesus, I know how they will feel. God will call them His children, no more war, or pain, or sin. Every one who comes to Jesus, God will surely let them in. So dare to dream that impossible dream, and one day you will see. That the greatest wealth in heaven above will come back for you and me.

Are You Surprised

It will happen in a moment, in the twinkle of an eye. Millions of people will disappear, and no one will know why. The entire world will be caught by surprise, and totally unaware. One moment we are with them, the next we are not there. The world is brought into instant panic, and no one has a clue. With the entire world having missing people, no one will know what to do. There are riots happening everywhere, with looting on the rise. Surely, this was unexpected, catching everyone by surprise. While on the other side of glory, a group is ushered in. These are the ones who were saved be grace, and redeemed of all their sin. At first, they all were startled, by the changes they went through. But as they surveyed the site before them, they immediately knew what to do. One by one, they fell down on their knees, worshiping before the King. All of heaven began to join them, and angels began to sing. All the saints in heaven stepped forward, and bowed before Him too. Just like a mighty chorus, everyone knew what to do. They sang a song of thanksgiving to Him, one of Honor and Glory and Praise. Hands were lifted and hearts were poured out, to the wonderful Ancient of Days. When this worship had finally ended, and the crowd stood to their feet. All of them were finally greeted, by the ones they have longed to meet. Jesus spoke to all of them, and welcomed them above. Then all the people were filled inside, with His unconditional Love.

It Is Him

One day we will step out of this earthly body, and then we will finally be free. We will lay aside this carnal tent, to enter eternity. Some may wish they could return, to that old familiar space. Anything at all that will get them out, of that evil hellish place. But those who gave their lives to Jesus will leave behind despair. They will quickly leave that earthly realm, and the trash that they left there. They will step into their brand new body, glorified and clean. It will be so perfect they will stand in awe, at a sight they have never seen. Seeing their shining bodies, they will be surprised as they start to dim. For a radiant light will then step forward, and they will know that it is Him. Jesus will come and take hold of their hand, and say welcome home my friend. Enter in to My Father's rest, where your life will never end. Then you will see the real you, like you have never seen before. All the saints of God will let out a shout, as you step through heavens door.

Catch Me Away

It was a gray and foggy day, and myself I harbored doubt. If this is how I will spend my life, would I ever make it out? So I decided at an early age to try to do my best. But I failed this task so many times; it was like an endless losing test. Whatever I put my hand to do seemed to always come out wrong. Yet I played that game so many times, it was like an old familiar song. When I was down in my pit of despair, there was no one who could talk me out. Then I would go into a pity party, where I could not release my doubt. As the years went by and my emptiness grew, there was a void within my heart. I knew there was something I needed desperately, but did not know where to start. Then one day I was called to the floor, so I rose to take my stand. I was face to face with destiny, when I saw His outstretched hand. As I peered into those nail print hands, He said are you ready to leave your doubt? For only by putting your trust in Me, will you ever find the way out. I reached out to the Savior, and fell before His feet. He laid a hand upon me, and my life became complete. Then He told me not to fear, for I had finally made it in. All my past was washed away, and He forgave me of all my sin. Then as He turned to go back to Heaven, He turned with a smile to say; trust in Me with all your heart. For soon, I will catch you away.

COME LORD JESUS

There is a day that is drawing near, a day I have longed to see. When raptured saints all meet in the air, which is where I want to be. Jesus will say come My beloved, and take hold of My hand. Then I will guide you through the narrow door, into the holy land. With trouble mounting everywhere, it is time to understand. That Jesus Christ will soon be here, salvation is at hand. There are wars and even talk of wars, with evil on the rise. Yet to all who know the word of God, this should come as no surprise. Some people do not realize how close the end may be. Where you may not get a second chance to have Jesus set you free. Do not wait for the tribulation, or when the mark is here. Invite the Lord into your heart, for salvation draweth near. Don't hold to evil living, and do not keep your hidden sin. For Jesus paid for everyone, and life He ushered in. The choice is now before you, and your reward is what you have sown. You can be saved for all of eternity, or you can suffer all alone.

My Life

When I have finally finished this life, and my Lord calls me away. I wonder what people will think of me, I am curious of what they will say? Will they say I was a good man who gave all that he had? Or will they only remember my wicked past, the one where I was always bad? Will they cry and mourn with a personal loss, or will it bring them sweet release. Well I suppose it really does not matter, for I will finally be at peace. You see your life is just a testimony, a book the world will see. Yet even when I try to hide it, they see the real me. If they find out I am a believer in Jesus, they watch this living book. Then whenever they see me make a mistake, it gets them all to look. I hear them say, oh look at you, who are holier then thou. You claim to be a Christian, but man look at you now. They examine all your faults and sins, and broadcast what they see. If he were really a believer in Christ, then he would not be acting like me. Well thankfully, we are saved by grace, and God has forgiven our sin. So we do not have to feel guilty, when they bring it up again. But while you are in this wicked world, they search for Jesus in you. So keep your eyes on our Lord and Savior no matter what others do. Then when it is time to leave this life, it will not matter what others say. When God decides to close the book of your life, a new one will start that day.

I Am Finally Home

That final stretch of life's journey ends, and you are no longer in this land. To a place, you have never been before, in His presence you now stand. You have reached your final destiny, and are in awe at what you find. To realize you are in a different place, but an even better kind. You do not feel pain any more, and inside you have no hurt. The flesh you have is made brand new, a kind not made of dirt. With a love that permeates your being, you are startled at its touch. You wonder where the pain all went, those ones that hurt so much. Then you hear the roar of thunder, as brightness fills the sky. You try to move as the place grows brighter, but you cannot and wonder why. Then you find you are standing in a city, filled with brilliant light. You are unable to speak a single word, as you gaze upon this wonderful sight. There before you is a beautiful throne, one with angels and elders standing by. You are beholding the face of the One on the throne, with a tear falling from your eye. Many crowns are thrown at His feet, and everyone there starts to bow. You hear Him speak like the sound of thunder, my child come here to Me now. Slowly you start to move closer to His light, as He reaches to wipe away that tear. Then He says welcome My good and faithful servant, come closer you have nothing to fear. For now that you have overcome, and done your very best. I have washed away your sins forever now enter into My rest. So you enter into His golden city, straight past the pearled gate. Down streets of gold that look like glass, where friends and family wait. They take you to a mansion, overwhelmed you praise the Lord. For you see the Father has kept His promise, and given you your reward. Then you come to a stop, as Jesus speaks, the saints all start to sing. Glory to God in the highest, worthy is our King. Then you realize how much He loves you, Jesus never let you alone, He was preparing a place for you in heaven, so rejoice you are finally home.

THE MARRIAGE SUPPER

One day the trumpet will blow from heaven, and our Lord will come down with a shout. At first, the dead in Christ will rise, and then every Christian will go out. Then on the shores of heaven, what a reunion there will be. For all our friends and loved ones, will be there for us to see. There will be plenty of time to reminisce, and to see the sights above. You cannot explain this kind of grace, His unconditional love. You will find angels, elders, and cherubim there, with so many sights to see. Just standing there on streets of gold, with my family there with me. After we have seen these wonderful things, and our reunion is finally done. The object of all our deepest desire, Will appear brighter then any sun. Jesus in all of His glory, the one we have waited to behold. Will be standing there before us, brighter then the purest gold. One by one, we will come before Him, and He will wipe our tears away. Joy will begin to fill our hearts, to hear our Savior say. I am glad to call you brethren; you have made it through each trial and test. I have prepared a special place for you, to receive the very best. Now come set down at My table, the food is always free. This is the day I have been waiting for, just to have you here with Me. Please set down at this wedding feast, and enjoy everything you see. For now, you will share with Me in My glory, and together we will always be. Nothing will separate you from My Love, and I am glad to call you friend. Now you will have eternal life, a future that will never end. So enjoy this feast before you, and remember why you are free. There was a time when you were lost, but you put your faith in Me.

Can't Wait

We are standing in a moment of time, awaiting the journey home. Walking this earth, without any hope so empty and alone. Babies are born and people are dieing, and some think their life is a joke. But will you see them laughing, when their heart beats its final stroke? Your life can be either full or empty; the choice is up to you. You have many choices to make in your life that will depend on what you do. You can do what everyone else is doing, by trying to keep the beat. Yet that will never bring you peace, or make your life complete. Nothing can fill that void you have, the one you feel within. This world has nothing to offer you, only emptiness, filled with sin. But when mortal life ends and death comes for you, and tries to take your soul. It will place its cold dark hand on you, and refuse to let you go. Now you are just a moment, and time may be on your side. But don't miss the road that leads to heaven, for that road to hell is wide. Then when you walk through the shadow of death, you will not have anything to fear. For as you call on the name of Jesus, your salvation will be here.

ARK OF SAFETY

My Lord it seems like everything's ready, for Your return again. There is trouble rising everywhere, and the earth is full of sin. People are starting to panic, at the trouble that they see. Those who do not know You are not certain what tomorrow will be. The gospel is being preached on the airwaves, it is reaching every land. They preach it in every language so that everyone will understand. Some are expecting a new revival, while others simply wait. Children today seem out of control, and their parents teach them to hate. What was it like when Noah built the ark; I wonder if his day was the same? How about Lot in wicked Sodom are we playing that evil game? My Lord I feel Your closeness, as You stand at the door and wait. For the word to come from the Father, and You step through heavens gate. How much more will we have to endure, how much longer will this last. Before You call the saints to heaven, and make the present past. Well we know how much You love us, for You came to save us all. But it sure will be so wonderful, joining the millions who hear Your call. Though it seems like there is not any hope, all our faith we place in You. So when You come to destroy all evil, You will make this earth brand new. Every day we wait for You Lord, and we are always watching too. We are waiting patiently for Your soon return, because Lord we all Love You.

Look Up

Some where in that place called heaven, there is a joy that is complete. Where the saints who went ahead of us are kneeling at Jesus feet. They are not thinking about you and me, for they finally have peace at last. All of us are in God's hands, future present, and past. But down here, we do not feel that peace, for our joy is not complete. That is why when God touches us His Love is oh so sweet. Still we have to face another day, which may bring us many trials. So like little children we cry out to heaven, and that is when Jesus smiles. For when we keep our eyes on our problems, they will start to overwhelm. So like a Sailor who is lost at sea, let Jesus take the helm. He can lead you away from danger, and speak into your storm. Just let the Potter mold and shape you, to see what He can form. You still may have disappointments, but do not worry and do not hide. For that devil cannot touch you, with Jesus on your side. So carry on your Christian walk, bring the Lord to those you meet. Keep your eyes looking up to heaven, and your life will be complete.

His Love

Our God He feeds the tiny birds, and He hears when people pray. With millions of voices all lifted at once, He can hear each word they say. The mountains are formed before Him, and storms are held at bay. With all the stars, He placed in the heavens, that is where they will always stay. When you are feeling all alone, and you think you, have no one to care. Just remember He has His eyes on you, speak to Him He is there. Tell Him why you are hurting inside, and remember He loves us all. Your problem may seem too big to fix, but for Him it is rather small. So call on the One that is able to help, or your problem may never go. Open your heart to our wonderful God, and remember He loves you so. You may think your world is crashing, and it may seem like there is no way out. That is only because you have lost your hope, and replaced your faith with doubt. Now is the time to change your mind be still and you will see. That God is bigger then any problem, that could come to you or me. Put your faith in action, and believe in God above. For every time He looks at His children, His heart is filled with love. Always remember that you are not alone, no matter how difficult life may be. God gave you His ultimate Love and Jesus set us free.

HOME SICK

The day I gave my heart to Christ, He filled my heart with love. It was God who chose to forgive my sins, by sending His Son from above. I asked the Lord to come into my heart to save my wretched soul. So that I could live in His wonderful kingdom, and never again have to go. Sometimes when I think of heaven, tears begin to fill my eyes. Yet I know that one day He will call us to heaven, for He hears our homesick cries. I think of the people who have gone on before us, how wonderful their new life must be. To be standing in heaven with Jesus, or maybe talking to my loved ones about me. I wonder sometimes just how it will be, when I finally enter that place. Will I fall on my knees when I finally see Jesus, with tears rolling down my face? Will my family be there to welcome me in, or will it be others who show me around? What will it be like to finally see Jesus, while standing on holy ground? All of those things bring joy to my heart, to know that the mystery will be through. When God calls me home, I will be there with your loved ones. Then I will tell them that you are coming too.

Paradise Today

There before my very eyes, I saw a bright and shining light. It had a kind of brilliance, and I was drawn to this wonderful sight. Then as it came even closer, I saw an outline of a man. He wore a robe so shiny and white, with scars near the top of His hands. I was shaken by this vision, and the power of this light. But as He turned and smiled to me, I knew it would be all right. A burst of love flowed through my being, and I felt like I was changed. It was as if every part of my earthly body was being slowly rearranged. He spoke with words that sounded like thunder, I felt wind blow through my soul. Sickness, sin and all evil were gone, and now I stood there whole. I had no desire to leave this place, as His glory produced a glow. He spoke no word of explanation, yet some how He let me know. Then He turned to walk away, and like diamonds that shine so bright. The glory of this brilliant Host now drew me to that light. We stepped up to those massive gates, and I heard Him speak again. He said welcome good and faithful servant and He motioned for me to go in. Then for a moment, I began to cry, but He wiped my tears away He said, remember I promised that when you believed, you would be in paradise with Me today.

Who Is Able

Who is able to ascend in to heaven? The ones whose hearts, are pure and clean. Where God will welcome them into glory, a place no human has seen. Where angels, and elders and all God's creation, are pure, and holy, and bright. The reflection of an all powerful God, who emanates with radiant light. He pours out His love in a Supernatural way, and speaks in a thunderous tone. Yet all of His creation knows they are loved, for He will never leave them alone. His power is one that no one can match, with wisdom to high to contain. So wise that no person could comprehend, for His knowledge would drive them insane. No one comes close to His all knowing ways, and His mercy is new every day. He speaks and all listen, He commands and it is done, and everything moves out of His way. He is gentle and loving and He cares for His children, and He never goes back on His word. For whatever He speaks will not return void, His message will always be heard. He is a powerful God and a loving Father, and One who will always supply. He is always there to meet every need, and you can believe Him He will never lie. The part that I love the most about Him is the mercy that He allows me to see. With a broken heart and tears in His eyes, He died so that I would be free. There upon that wooden cross, a way to heaven was found. For He saved my soul from a forever in hell, and turned my future around. So do you still wish to know who can ascend into heaven? Well it is rather plain to see, for I will ascend in to heaven, when my Jesus comes back for me.

HEAVENLY HOME

There will not be any need for hospitals in heaven, no medicine, or needles that stick. No more, need of a doctor's advice, for no one will ever get sick. No cars or buses, trains or planes, nothing that pollutes the air. For travel will happen in a moment, one thought and you will be there. Yet heaven will not be our home forever, for a new earth, our God will create. This is where His holy city will be, a place so awesome and great. There will be no more sea to take up space, for this earth will be changed and made new. I wonder if it will be like back in the beginning, watered by the morning dew. No more darkness in His city, and there is one thing that is the best. We will not have to wait a moment, to enter into His rest. With no more pain and no more hunger, for God will comfort and care. Just ask and He will give to you, call out and He will be there. With no more worry and no more fear, and no more sad goodbyes. God will wipe our tears away, and answer all of our cries. Many changes we will go through, but we will always feel His joy and love. God will be here with all of His children, just as it is in heaven above. The things that we now take for granted, in His kingdom they will not be. Walking with Jesus in the cool of the day, will be good enough for me. I will not need this earthly treasure, no power or physical care. For everything, we will ever need, we will have with Jesus there. Every thing He has given to us, He is the One who will always provide. For nothing can separate us from the love of God, we have Jesus on our side.

A Shout

One day we will meet in heaven, we will walk on streets of gold. We will see the saints who went before us, those patriarchs of old. We may hear King David sing the psalms, or see Paul as he preaches the word. We may even hear from Abraham, to learn of stories we have heard. Then we will walk to the river of life, with trees on either side. You may eat the fruit that grows on them, but it will be up to you to decide. So many sights and wondrous things, we will be taken back by surprise. All this beauty just lets us see, our God is awesome and wise. As you take a drink from the purest river, it will taste so fresh and clear. Then we will hear the angels proclaim, rejoice for the Lamb is here. The brightness of His glory will cause all radiance to grow dim. Then in holy reverence and honor, we will hear Moses say it is Him. There before our very eyes Jesus will appear. He will reach for us with love in His heart, and that love will draw us near. Then we will know that we are safe, and alive forever more. For the city of God will always be open, and no one will close that door.

That Name

When you have gone, through another trial, and it seems like it is finally through. Another one comes around the corner, and gets the best of you. You start to wonder why these things are happening, and you think this cannot be fair. Just keep in mind, who that tempter is, he is called the prince of the power of the air. Well we have a King who can conquer this foe. Yet when we are temped, we fall for his game. And when we are faced with another trial, we forget to call on the Name. There is power in the name of Jesus that can set the captive free. It can cause the earth to tremble, and can make the enemy flee. It will set your trials at liberty, and that fallen prince will run. When he see's that we have had enough, and our weapon is God's Son. Then all of the darkness that has settled around us will start to fade away. Then we will have the victory at last, when we remember it is time to pray. By calling upon the name of Jesus, the Lord will not let us down. He will hit that enemy with such a force; there will be nothing left but the ground.

THE WORD OF LIFE

The only thing they saw that day, were the crossbeams and the nails. No one understood what was being spoken; it was drown out by their angry wails. They did not look deep into His eyes, to see the love that was there. All they could see was a dieing man, and no one would even care. Here hanging on this man made cross, hung the Savior and God of all. Here the sacrifice would now be made, to remove the curse of the law. Yet still in their rage and anger, while walking in their pride. They were blinded to what awaited them, over on the other side. So violently, they took their stand, without caring what it would cost. They chose the law of sin and death, which showed them they were lost. Still God in all of His mercy, would remove this deadly stain. When His Son said It Is Finished, even death could not remain. At another place in the temple, the veil was torn in two. Then the God of heaven reached down His grace and whispered, I LOVE YOU.

NOT I WHO LIVES

The thunder crashed with lighting flashing, while darkness covered the land. There upon a roman cross, the world hung in God's hand. Beaten and bleeding in the sight of all man, the source of all life now died. Paying for the sins of the entire world, by being crucified. With every drop of blood He gave, all sin would be washed away. Paid in full to every sinner, who was crucified with Him that day. Now all who believed in His sacrifice would die with Him on that tree. To accept the Lamb supplied by God, that would set the sinner free. Now if you want your sins forgiven, you must call upon His name. Do not allow that old man back, or you will always be the same. If your sinful nature was put to death, it was hung upon that cross. Placed upon the Lamb of God, with the entire price it cost. God was there hanging in your stead, and paid our penalty on that tree. So that every person could be forgiven, who came to Calvary. Even though no good is in my flesh, and my two natures are at war you see. It is not I who lives my friend; it is Christ who lives in me.

God's Love For Us

If a bird can fall down from the sky, and never leave God's sight. It shows how much He cares for them He watches them in flight. How about the beautiful flowers, with fragrance that fills the air. He gives them all a special touch, providing them with care. Then think about the stars at night how He placed them in the sky above. So that every time that we looked up, we would see His wondrous love. Let us now consider the object of His plan. After planting a garden and making it beautiful, He then created man. He placed him in the garden, to till and take care of this place. But man listened to the serpent, and forgot about God's glory and grace. Man and woman were lost in sin, and their fellowship with the Father was done. Yet God had a plan to redeem His creation, by sending His Only Son. The people saw a brilliant light that shined for the world to see. Everyone who received His grace would find they could be set free. Evil tried to ruin this plan, to stop redemptions flow. While every time they stood in the way, the Gospel would always grow. Here God's Son hung on that cross, beaten and almost dead. He whispered ever so softly, and many heard the words He said. The fate of the world was in His hands; the penalty had to be paid. When He said that 'It Is Finished' the payment then was made. The plan of God was carried out each detail was in place. So that someday we could live with Him, to see Him face to face. So when you wonder if God really loves you, remember what you could have lost. Sin required the payment of death, and Jesus paid the cost. So does He really love us, just open your heart and see, when Jesus died upon that cross, He was thinking of you and me.

Now Is The Time

There is a day that is coming soon, when Jesus will sit on a throne. He will summons those to judgment, for the deeds, which they have sown. They will all have their excuses, for those things, which they have done. Yet nothing will stop that judgment, when they stand before God's Son. Most will say they are sorry, they will plead for His mercy and grace. Jesus will be listening to each one of them, with tears rolling down His face. All of them heard about salvation, when it was offered freely then. Now they will have to pay the debt, for their unrepented sin. Some will even ask for proof, of those things, which they have done. Jesus will open the book of their life, and show them one by one. There will be no more time to get right with God, when you stand before the King. When Christ sits down upon that throne, many will feel deaths sting. Those who always had the answer to all that life was about are now awaiting judgment, and no one has any doubt. They know it will soon be over, as they kneel before the Lord. The payment for sin is way too high, for any sinner to afford. Then He will open the final book, and they will know He was no liar. For if their name is not written in His book, He will say to them lake of fire. When this final judgment is over, He will stand and leave this place. Those who were thrown to the lake of fire will never again see His face. I know you may not like what you are hearing, and your view may never budge. But just keep in mind; He can now become your Savior. If you wait, He will be your Judge.

HOLY GHOST POWER

They were waiting in the upper room, for the promise of the Lord. No one knew of what would be coming, yet they were praying in one accord. All of them were quietly deciding, just who would take Judas's place. He would have to be someone, who was there from the beginning, and filled with God's love and grace. As these saints were quietly praying, and their praises were lifted higher. The Holy Spirit blew into the room, like cloven tongues of fire. Every person with no distinction began to speak a new word. The people, who gathered in town that day, were wondering at what they heard. Then as the Spirit began to move, on those who would believe. Many gifts were given that day, to all who had faith to receive. They would lay their hands on people who were sick, and see them become brand new. With power, they would open blinded eyes, and cast out demons too. One thing that all the believers had, that was different from the rest. They were led by the Holy Spirit, and His leading was the best. Always praying and full of joy, they had all things in common too. Every believer can have this joy, because Jesus lives in you. All those things that they once did, every Christian can do the same. If you place your faith in Jesus, believing in His name. Just ask the Father for anything, He will give it all to you. As long as it lines up with His word, and honors Jesus too. There is power in the name of Jesus, just speak it you will see. As blinded eyes are opened and demons start to flee. It is not because you have all the power, or anything you have done. It is because you speak in the name of Jesus, the power is God's Son. So fill up on that Holy Ghost power, and the enemy will stop his attack. For when you stand in the hottest battle, remember Jesus has your back.

His Amazing Grace

While walking in the Spirit one day, I was startled by the things I saw. There was evil lurking everywhere, and certainly tempting all. There were people sinning without even caring, and none of them feeling ashamed. I also saw people who were resisting this evil; they were calling on Jesus name. Darkness surrounded those who were sinning, but a light shined on all who received. Those who were once in the shadow of darkness came to the light, as they believed. Still inside the darkness where sin would then appear, it would take hold of the fearful and weak. The light would then shine like the sun in its glory, while a thunderous voice would then speak. Those who had faith and followed the Son were bathed in His glorious light. They would return to the darkness and come out with another, like daytime overpowering the night. On and on like a spiritual war, where some are removed from the flame. Brought to the light and cleansed of their sin, to never again be the same. I turned around to leave that place, and a voice called out from the light. Saying put on your armor, and take up your weapon then join in this spiritual fight. For this darkness is only a shadow, that will flee when it comes close to the light. Yet it cannot stand up to the righteous, for this brightness is one it cannot fight. Take the light of the gospel of Christ, and then go into that darkened place. Lead someone out of their life filled with sin, and bring them to My Amazing Grace.

POWER IN HIS WORD

There is a sweet anointing, on those who here God's call. They serve the Lord wherever He leads them, and are ready to give their all. They never leave home without the Word; they take it wherever they go. When they are asked to pray for someone they let God's anointing flow. People are healed, and some are set free, and loosed from years of shame. His power goes out from those who believe, as they pray in His wonderful name. As you speak the name of Jesus, demons have to flee. When you speak His name in power and authority, blinded eyes will see. The lame will walk and the dead will be raised, by the power of God's Son. It can move a mountain or calm the sea, and change lives when the praying is done. There is explosive power God gives to believers, who pray in Jesus name. They have tasted of the glory of the one true God, and will never again be the same. God has equipped us for a special purpose, to heal to deliver and set free. He lives in every believer, which is where He will always be. So take the word like a flaming sword, and speak in power and might. Let the name of Jesus, be your weapon day or night. Then the enemy will know for certain, this believer will not back down. For when you stand on the word of God, you are standing on Holy Ground.

WORRY NOT

Worrying is a bad disease, and deadly it can be. Some people don't worry part of the time they worry constantly. With all the time, they waste each day, worrying about things they fear. Their mind is clouded with worrying, and they worry when everything is clear. Some worry for no reason, even when nothing can be done. They worry until they are feeling sick, and wonder why their healing will not come. With all the time that is lost to worrying, these people are bound by fear. You can bet that when their worrying starts, that old devil is somewhere near. You need to turn to God with your troubles, to get the answer's that are plain to see. Stop your worrying for nothing, and let Jesus set you free. You know that He will solve your problems, and the worrying will be done. Just bring them all to the One who cares, Jesus Christ God's Son. So put your faith in action, and you will be worry free. The Lord can fix any problem you have, trust Him and you will see. Take your faith and cast out fear, let go of the problems you have got. Cast your cares upon the Lord, have faith, and worry not.

With My Blood

A light once shined upon this earth, everywhere man would be. The word then traveled from coast to coast, and across the deepest sea. Nothing could stop this manifested glory, it would continue until everyone knew. For God had a plan, to bring redemption to all, that would make each person new. This love would cause even hard hearts to fail, and cause evil to shudder and flee. Yet it had to be simple, so that all could receive and this gift would have to be free. Now this was quite a problem, how all sins could be removed without loss? How could a sinner be completely forgiven, and why would God die on a cross. This plan of perfection, no one else could complete a plan only He could fulfill. It required His grace, and unconditional love, a plan to accomplish His will. No man on earth could complete this task, for he would have to be sinless and pure. For with horrible pain and great suffering, this plan only God could endure. As He hung on a cross, the curse would be broken, while heaven and earth held its breath. Now came the time to fulfill this great plan, to witness all sin put to death. Darkness stood ready to see this plan fail, they were sure they would see He was done. Then to their surprise, they were frozen with fear, for out from the grave walked God's Son. The saints that were dead were standing there with Him. They knew that this day they would dread. For they witnessed Him placed in a borrowed tomb, but now He is alive and not dead. The light of God overpowered the darkness, and the devil was stripped of his glee. Then Jesus spoke out with power in His words, "with My blood they belong to Me."

Olden Days

Every older generation has their good old days, the wonderful times they have spent. Days where things were simple and free, I wonder where all those good old days went. You remember how times were tough on everyone, but you always found a way. Yet now life seems so different, as you enter this modern day. Everyone has their stories to tell; as they remember all the struggles, they went through. As the years moved on those hard times were gone and you remembered how they strengthened you. Sometimes we bring up pleasant times, those moments we love to share. Yet no one likes to hear of our joy because frankly, they were not there. So with all the time we spend on earth, we watch as another day flies past. Where no one knows what the next day will bring, or even if their life will last. Will we share those other old time stories, or will we say our last goodbye? Will anyone even remember us, or even feel sad or cry? Well the bible says we will all live again, some in heaven and others in hell. You may not even be aware of this, with all the stories that you tell. God says that He loves all of us, which is why He sent His Son. This is not a made up story, He came to die for everyone. There is no one living who has not sinned, all bare their guilt and shame. But thanks to God, we can be forgiven, by calling on Jesus name. But His story did not end in death you see Jesus rose again. Now those who ask Him to forgive them will be free from all their sin. You can still tell your stories of those good old days, what a great way to spend your day. Yet take a moment to call on Jesus, just bow your head, and pray. Ask the Lord to save your soul, and to wash away your sin. He will come and live inside you, and you will never be the same again. Just tell Him you are sorry; then trust Him to set you free. Then you will have a story to tell, like the one He gave to me. It will be a story about the Son of God, who is living in your heart. A person who chose to believe the truth, and willing to do his part. Then if this should be your final day, your story will then unfold. About a sinner who was finally saved by Jesus, the greatest story you ever told.

Too religious

There is something that really bothers me, those tricks the enemy will use. He causes people to lose their souls, by the wicked ways they choose. Like saying, it is only a little lie that the Lord will overlook. Yet God says telling lies is wrong, it is written in His book. How about the evil traits, like the things that are just not seen. The ones that go unnoticed like plain old gossiping. Gossip spreads the devils lies, like lightening that flashes so quick. When you see a Christian gossiping, it is enough to make you sick. What about those who point out sin, who never miss another's fault. They only spot the other person's sin, while theirs is an occult. They walk around with their halos showing, while their horns are hidden away. Then when they see the crowd around, that is when they are ready to pray. They start to preach when no one asks them to; they have power in their pride. Yet let a person ask for a handout, and these saints will run and hide. All these people say that they know Jesus; still I wonder how they would feel. If someone pointed out their sin, and said their faith was not real. Some of them are very sincere, yet they are sincerely wrong. They would like everyone to believe that they are holy, by playing the same old song. When you think that you are better then others, there is something you should know. You have been a baby Christian for years, and it is time for you to grow. Stop pointing your finger at other people, oh you who have no sin. If you think that you know more then God, then give the cross a spin. Let someone nail your hands and feet, then die and resurrect. Then to you my holy brother, we will all give you respect. Still you can never take the place of Jesus, and He will always be the king. Jesus is the Judge of everyone, and He knows everything. So the next time that you feel like judging, grab that bible down from the shelf. It tells you not to judge others, or you will bring judgment on yourself. Just try to stop for one moment, and give that sinner some space. Let Jesus move upon their heart, He will give that soul His grace. Then all the glory will go to God, they will be saved there is no doubt. Just try to remember that Jesus is the Savior, and throw your religion out.

Letter To Dad

My Lord you know what is in our heart, and you know the way we feel. Problems come and we start to worry, yet the outcome was never real. Please help us Lord to trust in You, and place fear beneath our feet. Let our faith be magnified, so our joy will be complete. Sometimes we wonder what tomorrow will bring, even before the day is through. Yet what we need is super faith, to put our trust in You. It is not that we do not believe Your word; we are just so used to defeat. Please help us Lord to turn around, and make our victory so sweet. Show us how to walk by faith, and not by what is in sight. Then if we should start to struggle a little, please lift us with Your might. I know my Lord I still may fail, and my heart may break within. Yet I trust You Lord to walk with me, until I no longer sin. If I should fail, and fall flat on my face, and feel like my life is through. Then give me strength to call for help, until I am safe with You. There is one thing I am certain of, that promise I have always had. That I am your child and You love me so, and You will always be my Dad.

You Are Forgiven

They brought her to the Savior, their judgment so complete. Knowing that she was guilty, they threw her at His feet. Another soul caught in their vicious web just to see what He would do. Yet Jesus knelt down and He wrote on the ground, as their wicked anger grew. Teacher they said, this woman before You was taken in unlawful sin. Our law says we must stone her to death, so she cannot do it again. Jesus stood up and He looked at her, and saw a sinner all alone. He turned and said you who have never sinned, be the first to cast a stone. One by one they turned away, leaving their stone's there on the ground. Then He asked her, where are your accusers? Yet none of them could be found. Tears of repentance filled her eyes, as she felt His loving grace. No sweeter joy to know you are forgiven, and to see it in His face. Go He said, you are forgiven, do not continue as before. Then He said you have been forgiven, now go, and sin no more.

FAITH ALONE

My Father please forgive me for wandering from Your word. Forgive me for not listening, for Your voice I should have heard. Every time when all is fine, and I forget what I am called to do. I know my Father it cause's my grief, because I am not where I should be with You. Right now, the worrying I see myself doing is because I have caused this mess. When all I had to do was believe, and You would have done the rest. Sometimes I feel like my faith is weak, where I fret the things of tomorrow. It cause's me to grow weary inside, and brings me all kinds of sorrow. Sometimes I worry for those I love, the ones You have entrusted to my care. Sometimes I need to be reminded, that You are always there. I still have tears that are crying inside of me, when I cannot see any way out. That is when I know I am failing, when my faith is turned to doubt. Father I love you with all my heart, but sometimes my valley seems dry. Please fill me with joy and comfort my Lord, because your children should never cry. Give me the faith to carry on, even when everything is going all wrong. Help me to walk by faith alone, while lifting a worship song. Father please lead me to where you want me to be, when it is hard to hear Your call. You are my Healer, and my provider, Lord You are my All in All. Please lead me Father to that river of life, so I can drink and be thirsty no more. Change my heart, keep me close to You, until I meet You at heavens door. I want to grow and trust fully in You, to not fear what I am unable to complete. I will take my burdens and all of my cares, and lay them at Your feet.

Faith To Praise

Lord I lift my voice in praise, with hands lifted to Your throne. I wait and watch and listen always, for You to call us home. In this world, there is doom and gloom, but I am not afraid. For all my family trusts in You, and the promises You have made. Our hope is in Your wonderful care, knowing that we cannot lose. If it ever comes to making a choice, it is You that we will choose. For if a person gains the entire world, yet forsakes Your loving call. He will condemn his soul for eternity, and surely lose it all. Money will never save us, and its pleasure just will not last. For the world is quickly passing away, with judgment approaching fast. So help us Lord to keep our eyes on You, safe in Your loving care. Until we leave this earth below, and meet You in the air. Fill us with Your Holy Spirit, and Lord always keep us true. For we place our faith in the Word of God, knowing someday we will be with You.

Greater Is He

Somewhere in the spiritual realm, a war is being waged. demons are trying to stop the blessings, where angels are being engaged. They fight in this spiritual battle, for the souls of unsaved man. To bring the answers that they are seeking, that will help them to understand. Still the gospel of the great God above is advancing ahead everyday. Nothing can stop the Word of God; no evil will stand in the way. Still this darkness is all around, and continues to enter the fight. Many souls have heard the gospel, and moved closer to the light. Still the enemy of redemption is trying to cloud their mind. With the seeds of grace planted everywhere, just waiting for them to find. One sinner saved and angels rejoice, and yet another one falls for the lie. They only see death as the final way out; thinking they are free when they die. Here is a world where this unseen battle, is being waged for every man. Yet God has all their futures, He holds them in His hand. Evil can never stand up to His might, for none can compare to His power. God has determined everyone's fate, and they are waiting until that final hour. One day soon all will bow to the Lord, and be judged in that final day. Those who are lost will have no defense, as they are finally led away. Our fight is not against flesh and blood, it is a battle that is already won. Jesus has conquered death, hell, and the grave, so the victory is already done. So do not be afraid of those who are perishing, into the fire they will one day be hurled. For greater is He who lives in us, then he that lives in this world.

White Throne Judgment

They all were waiting for the judgment to begin, as the throne was set in place. Thousands and thousands were waiting their turns, to see Him face to face. Yet these would stand in judgment, for the things, which they had done. They were here for just one reason, for rejecting God's Holy Son. As the door to the kingdom was opened, the King came and sat down on His throne. The ones, who stood before Him, were shaken and all alone. No one stood up in their defense and no price would let them get in. They were there for only one purpose, to be judged for all their sin. One by one, they all came forward and the book of their life was read. Many had done some real great things but to their shame all, their works were dead. Then He searched to see if their name was written in His book. They all hoped to escape this judgment, as He took one final look. Then if their name was blotted out, or not written there at all. His judgment rendered them guilty, for they missed the Saviors call. Every soul condemned that day, who rejected His gift of grace. Were thrown alive into the lake of fire, to never again see His face. Yet just before they were sentenced, they had to kneel at His feet. To call Him the King of Kings and Lord of Lord's, before their judgment was complete. Then as this final judgment was over, with those souls condemned that day. The Judge stood up from His throne of judgment, and wiped His tears away. The saints will know that this judgment is over, for eternity will finally begin. They will live forever with Jesus, completely free of sin.

WILL YOU BE THERE

Will you be at the bema seat, to receive a special crown? Or will you be at the white throne judgment, where all your sins will be found? Will you hear Jesus say you are welcome My child, enter eternal rest. Or will you find that you are guilty, even though you did your best? You see God is not weighing your deeds on a scale, where your good outweigh the bad. He is not looking at your church attendance, or the friends that you have had. His judgment will truly be righteous, not by things that you have done. The only thing that will matter then is if you gave your life to His Son. Jesus said that, He is the Way and no other way will do. So if you find that you are standing in judgment, then it is only because of you. God has given Him the name above all names, and no other has the power to save. You have to be saved by Jesus alone, and the sacrifice He gave. The time we have on earth is short, and the midnight hour is near. Give your heart to Jesus now, for soon He will be here. You can choose to be at the victory seat, where your reward will be so great. Or think you have all the time in the world, just to find out you were to late. God is not playing some cosmic game, where He is trying to raise the score. Yet when the time of grace is over, He will finally close that door. Then tribulation will come to all, who believed their salvation, they could earn. Yet at the judgment seat of Christ, their fate they will finally learn. Call on Jesus to save your soul, to wait you just cannot afford. Come meet Him at the bema seat, and receive a great reward. We are all here but a moment, like a vapor that is passing away. There is only one way you will make it to heaven, that is to accept the Lord today.

BOW AND CONFESS

God said that one day every knee would bow; all will kneel before His Son. Every tongue will confess Him as Lord and King, down to the very last one. Then as they bow before the King, He will call them all by name. Some will worship and praise Him, while others will stand in shame. Many will say they are sorry, they will say they did not know. He will say I never knew you, and then away from Him, they will go. There will be those who were once important, like presidents who believed they were great. They will try to plead their status, but then it will be too late. Even the devil will come before Him, he will bow and confess Jesus name. Then he will finally be led away, and thrown into that torturous flame. Those who refused to accept God's Son have now come before Him too late. Now they will be judged and forever suffer, for they have chosen the devils fate. Those who look into the eyes of the Lord will know their truth is out. They will finally believe it is over, and none of them will have any doubt. Then when the last person bows before Him, He will close His book at last. Then He will start a new future with the saints, and completely remove the past. All things new, and all things pure, and we will be forever in His sight. So do not waste another moment deciding, you could bow before Him tonight.

THE BATTLE

Spirits, elders, and living beings, all stand before the Lord. As one cries holy, holy, holy, all worship in one accord. A holy scroll is in the hand of Him, who is seated upon the throne. Yet only one person is worthy to open it, Jesus, and Him alone. Seven seals would be opened in heaven, to fulfill this end time plan. While one by one the wrath of God, will be poured out on sinful man. As every seal is being removed, the trouble on earth will begin. Seals, trumpets, and bowls of wrath, poured out for their love of sin. Yet up in heaven a multitude rejoices, as they worship before the King. Thousands and thousands all lifting their voices, everyone in heaven starts to sing. Blessing and glory wisdom, and thanksgiving, honor, and power and might. Be unto our God forever and ever, oh what a powerful sight. Then a door in heaven is opened, as Jesus mounts a snow white steed. Millions and millions fall in behind Him, with the King of Kings taking the lead. What a fearful sight for those on the earth, they look up to see His glory appear. Many cry to the mountains to fall on them, to hide them from the trouble that is here. The beast and his army are quickly defeated, by the Word as a two-edged sword. Yet not one of the saints ever raises a weapon, for the battle belongs to the Lord.

The Accuser

He is the accuser of the brethren; the one who destroys the saints. With his evil lies and accusations, what an ugly picture he paints. He spins his evil web of pain, while trying to destroy men's souls. He has no mercy on anyone, no matter where he goes. The one thing I am sure about, he has always been a liar. So when this deceiver has come to his end, God will throw him to the lake of fire. Now he roams around like a roaring lion, seeking whom he may devour. He sets his traps for the saints of God, while awaiting his final hour. The day is coming when this fallen angel will bow before the Lord. Then God will cast him into a place of torment, along with his evil hoard. Then all of his followers will finally see; that their leader was a fake. Still this will be the end for them, and they will follow him into that fiery lake. Then the smoke of their suffering and torment will rise up for all to see. All the saints will give the glory to God, for He has finally set us free. So the next time that devil brings up your past, all those lies that no one has heard. Just remind him of his future, it is written in God's Word.

THE PERFECT PRAYER

If I could pray the perfect prayer, it would start with all my love. I would tell my Father what I feel in my heart, and then lift it to Him above. I would focus all my inner thoughts on praise and worship too. Then I would say to my Father; Lord, I love and worship You. Then as I lifted my voice to Him, I would tell Him how my day was spent. If I have sinned in any way, to Him I would repent. Then God would hear this special prayer, with my hands raised to His throne. Where I would feel His holy presence and know I am not alone. Yet for me to have a perfect prayer in Spirit and in Truth the same. I would have to pray from within my heart, while lifting Jesus name. There is something to the name of Jesus that makes the oceans roar. It causes demons to flee in terror, and opens heavens door. When the Father hears that wonderful name, there is a smile on His face. Only His Son would die for His Father, to save the human race. So I know when I pray in that special name, my perfect prayer is heard. For He looks at me through the Blood of Jesus, as I lift up every word. Then as my prayer goes up before Him, it is seasoned with His grace. Just to hear the name of Jesus puts a smile on His face.

Holiest Washing

Well I have received the holiest washing, with all things inside me made whole. All the garments I have were cleansed by Lord Jesus, and by His blood, I am whiter then snow. Not one person on earth could ever come close to the suffering my Savior went through. All the pain and the torment that He had to bare, we are forgiven that is what He came to do. As the blood and the water flowed out from His side, the covenant He made would begin. All would be saved who were washed by His blood, to be free from the bondage of sin. No sin or sickness, death or disease will be anywhere around to be seen. For He cleansed me in the blood of redemption and now my life is, clean. He took the sin that stained my soul, and washed away all shame. With the precious blood of the Lamb of God, my life is not the same. The cleansing blood of my Savior, has washed away my past. Now I can live with my Lord forever, free from my sins at last.

THE DEADLY WOUND

Darkness filling the skies that day, upon a blood stained hill. Evil stood there like wild bulls, ready to make their kill. The curtain spread before the temple so man could not get in. Yet soon the blood would demand redemption by removing every sin. There upon that roman cross the hope of all man would die. Immortal words from the Author of life, "it is finished" they heard Him cry. The demons stood there full of joy, with sarcasm on their breath. Thinking that they had won the battle, as they witnessed Him put to death. The wind began to blow with force and the sky grew dark as night. The curtain of the temple that held man at bay was torn in everyone's sight. Surely, this was a Righteous man a roman soldier would say. Yet soon the world would see the truth of just what was on the way. Down in hell the enemy waited, they were rejoicing in this hour. They did not realize they were out of time; God soon would display His power. Thick clouds of gloom hung in the air, and their end would now arrive. As a powerful light exploded in hell, there was Jesus so alive. He grabbed the keys of death and hell then turned to walk away. Hell would now be sealed forever; those there would have to stay. He then stepped back into His body, as the earth slowly let out its breath. Behold the King the Son of God, has conquered sin and death. Memorial graves were opened that day and the righteous dead returned once more. Death had lost its powerful sting, as Jesus opened hells door. Then He rose up to heavens glory, to prepare a special place. So He could one day come to take them home, who have received His gift of grace. So keep in mind the battle is won and evil now rules no more. For Jesus delivered a deadly wound, and He crushed their foolish war.

WAITING FOR THE CALL

One day when I have finished my work and my time on earth is past. My mortal body will return to the earth, and I will be immortal at last. No longer will I feel any pain and no worry will rob my day. No sickness to hinder me any more, no nothing will stand in my way. It is all because I took the time to make Jesus the Lord of my life. I now look forward to eternity in heaven with my children and my wife. Jesus paid the ultimate price, to redeem my soul from deaths hold. He made the payment with His precious blood, which cost more, then silver or gold. Then He prepared a place for me, there in heaven up above. For the day when He will bring us there, to feel His wonderful love. So until my time is over here, no matter how long it may be. I will keep on waiting and keep on watching, for my Jesus to call for me.

Hope For The Hopeless

There is a place where people go, when they have no hope at all. A place where God will heal the pain, and never let them fall. Yet sometimes the cares and the struggles in life are able to get you down. Just keep on knocking, asking, and seeking until the Lord is found. Though we do not know what tomorrow will bring, there are plenty of things we must do. We can keep our heads above the water, with all the things that we go through. Our God is full of mercy and grace, and will guard the path we take. No matter how bad our day may seem, most of the problems are ones we make. There are many things that we neglect, like giving a helping hand. By thinking about the other person, we can begin to understand. That all our trouble can rob our hope and even steal our strength within. Yet going to that place with God, in faith we will always win. This place can be in your closet or beside your bed at night. It can be in your car or in a quiet room, wherever you are in His light. Just remember hope is knowing that our God will never lie. Lift your voice in prayer, and give the Lord a try. Then you will be in a place of peace, where God will make a way. For in your heart is where you can find Him, and He will be there every day.

FLEE ALL SIN

Sin is like a cancer that can darken this earthly realm. It can cause a person to worry for nothing, bring shame, and overwhelm. The seeds of total darkness grow from an evil place. It has to be dealt with and washed away; it has infected the human race. Yet when it is taken to the cross of Jesus, it is washed away instead. For under this precious flow of blood, the root of all sin is dead. When sin is brought to His cleansing blood, the stain is washed away. The light of the Lord will over power the darkness, where sin can never stay. Jesus shed His blood for all, to cleanse and make us new. So that one day we could join Him in heaven, and be with our Savior too. So if you are a brand new creation, then you are washed from all your sin. So keep yourself from darkness and let no evil in. Then the next time you are faced with evil, just remember how the devil fell. He trusted sin like a long lost friend, and it sentenced him to hell.

Jesus Freak

I am patiently waiting for Jesus, and no matter what you think of me. If He happens to come back this very moment, at His side is where I will be. I know you may think I am a Jesus freak, and my friend you may be right. Yet when my Lord comes back for me, I will be in His holy light. You can call me Holy Roller and choose to believe that too. Though when my big brother Jesus comes back, He may roll all over you. I know you think I am crazy and have really lost my head. Yet this is not some religious theory, my Jesus is not dead. It does not matter what you think of me, my friend I do not care. Because when my Savior calls my name, I will join Him in the air. So do not worry about me my friend, no matter how crazy it may be. When this earth becomes like the pit of hell, there will be no one to set you free. I plan to be with Jesus, those who stay here will be alone. You will not find us Jesus freaks here; you will then be on your own. So why not grab your bible, and do not wait until it is too late. You can have a place in heaven, where those holy rollers are at the gate. Then you will see I was not crazy, you will hear angels start to sing. Then you will become a Jesus freak too, when you meet my Lord and King.

Your Calling

Jesus said you are the light of the world that will shine for all to see. A reflection of the Master equipped for what you will be. Some will preach in pulpits while others evangelize. Still some will go to the poorest lands to comfort the hurting cries. Some will greet in churches or teach a child or two. It does not matter how great that calling, the Lord depends on you. Now you may tell a person today, that God wants to save their soul. Or you may be someone who prays by yourself, and still our God will know. For if, you give a glass of water to someone, and give it in a prophet's name. Then God will see a work being done, and reward you both the same. Or you may lay your hands on a sick person or be there to help someone in need. Yet every time you doing a good work, you are planting a holy seed. Our Lord has commissioned us to go into the world and to preach His holy word. It does not matter what calling you have, for it is your actions that are really heard. The world that we all go to, can be in such a mess. Yet God has given us the tools to succeed, and He will supply the rest. So it does not matter what you are doing for Jesus, no matter how small it may be. Just keep in mind how much He loves us, and every good thing He will see. We have to work while there is light and no work will go undone. For God loved this world with all of His heart, and the proof is Jesus His Son. He came to reconcile sinners and to wash away their sin. So that when He calls them all to heaven, they are sure to be welcomed in. so always remember you have a special calling, it can be big, or small that is true. Yet the thing that makes it very special is that God gave this calling to you.

The Actor

There is a person who acts religious, but he is religious unto himself. Every day but Sunday their religion is on the shelf. They would like the world to see them, the way they would like to be. Yet they have a heart full of wickedness and are way to blind to see. They never miss a meeting every time the church is open. For they think that someone will see their religion, which is what these folks are hoping. You will see them wave their holy gifts that all can see them give. But deep in their heart, they are stingy, and hoarding is how they live. You can tell these people are holy, for up front is where they will stand. So if the Pastor walks by them, he just may shake their hand. Oh but when it comes to dealing with sin, they are great at finding your fault. They do not care if you are wounded; they just rub on a little salt. Then if you tell them that they too are sinners, your seat had better be level. For they will lose their holiness in a moment, and you will think you met the devil. They know they are going to heaven, for they were first to stake their claim. Yet they are not sure where you are going, because your goodness is not the same. They raise their hands when the song gives the cue, and have mastered every word. Yet just ask them to explain the message preached, and it is like it was not heard. You can spot them when you get to church; they will always be the same. They have their own special group they are with, and they know each other's name. They are always where the action is, up front to get their part. They will worship God with all they have, except with their righteous heart. Well it is not wrong to want to be holy, and to give is worship indeed. Still you must never forget where you came from, or the reason you have been freed. When you took from the river of heaven, your body did not drink. So your flesh my friend makes you a sinner, no matter what you may think. The day you die your spirit and soul will depart to the Father it is true. But that body of flesh will go back to the ground for it cannot go with you. Then one day when the trumpet blows, that body will shoot up from the ground. It will be changed from mortal to immortal and your righteousness will then be found. There will be no more sin in your members, and holy you will truly be. Yet until we meet the Lord in the sky, just remember you are just like me. So the next time when you walk into church, just remember your no better then the rest. Show a person the love of Jesus, and then you will truly be blest.

From Time To Eternity

Time is the future, present, and past, a shadow of what you see. Time is a place where no one can stay, where some have longed to be. Time is a moment that has come and gone, a future that is turned to past. For time will come and then will go, an age that will not last. That is why we should use each second we have, to glory of our King. For no one knows what will happen tomorrow, or what the time will bring. Take each moment of time you have and use each minute wise. For if you stop to think things out, you discover just how time flies. The future clock is ticking and that moment will soon be here. You will not have time to look back on your past, for your future is drawing near. God has set a special day, when your time will then be through. Then time will turn to eternity, no time will be left for you. Yet do not forget how much He cares, about the amount of time you lose. He does not decide how we use that time; He leaves it to us to choose. So the time you spend in eternity, may bring you your desire. Or your time may be without God forever, suffering in the lake of fire.

INTO THE DEEPEST SEA

God gave me a special gift; it is one that made me free. He took my past and threw it behind Him, into the deepest sea. For I was a terrible person, my life was quite a mess. Yet God saw something special in me, and He loved me nonetheless. While the devil never lets me forget my past, or the way I used to be. He brings my sin up all the time, as he tries to ruin me. Then as I feel the sorrow, for those things, that I have done. God says I do not know your past; it was covered in the blood of my Son. Then I feel the heart of my Father; pour that cleansing blood on me. He tells me not to listen to that devil, for His Son Jesus set me free. The accusations of the devil, they surely will not last. For Jesus holds my future, while Satan brings up my past. So the next time that devil even says to me, just look what you have done. I will lift my voice and praise my Father, for sending Jesus His Son. No more will I let the sins of my past, be a part of life for me. For Jesus holds my future and that's why I am free.

Are You Really Poor

Being poor is not so bad, it is all where you begin. You see I can go into the poorest area and really fit right in. some people may make fun of me and no matter how that may sound. My clothes are more religious then theirs, for I wear Noah's hand me downs. Now some may laugh because I have no money, and wonder how does he live. Yet I do not mind their joking, I smile when they have to give. They may drive around in fancy cars and play tennis or golf for fun. Yet I am content to spend my time fishing, where my story is the biggest one. Being poor is not really so bad, at least you will not know greed. Remember that with all the bills coming in, you will always have something to read. Shopping is real easy I do not go where the price will soar. I just jump inside my running shoes and hit the local store. Well let me tell you about a friend I have, very wealthy but not like the rest. He visits me when I have nothing, and tells me I am the best. He does not care if you are rich or poor and like a brother that's the way He see's us. I love my friend because He first loved me, and my wonderful friend is Jesus.

GOD'S PURPOSE FOR ME

God gave me eyes to behold His glory, to see the wonderful things He made. He gave me a mind so that I could decide which foundation I would like laid. He gave me a nose to smell all His flowers, and ears just to hear should He call. He wanted us to be in His image, which is why He gave us it all. I have a mouth so that I can speak to Him, to confess Him as my Savior and King. He gave me two feet so I could jump with excitement as I lift up my voice and sing. He gave me two hands to put together a way of expressing my praise. I can use them to clap and do many things, and with my arms, these hands I can raise. On the inside of me, He gave me a heart, so that I can show Him just how I feel. Then He placed His Spirit in me, to show that His love is real. My Father gave me all of His love, in Jesus the One He holds dear. Who broke the hold that devil had on me; God released me from all my fear. All of the things that God has done for us cannot compare to the treasure He holds. We were wonderfully created for His special purpose, and He will show us when that purpose unfolds.

THE TITHE

My Holy Father in heaven, to Your storehouse I now come to give. Returning to You the tenth that I owe, for this very life I live. I know You will open the floodgates above, and pour blessings where I have no room to receive. Yet I am not here to test You Father, I do it because I believe. When it comes to me giving what I owe to You Lord, I fall short of the debt that I owe. So I will bring in the tithe, as I know that I should, in hopes that my faith will grow. I pray that the tenth that I bring in my Lord, will keep me from clinging to greed. For I know that giving is part of receiving, so Your blessings can meet every need. Please forgive me Lord for the times I have robbed You, by not supplying the food for Your shelve. I finally realized this great truth my Father I was only robbing myself. So help me Lord to return what is Yours, all the things that belong to You. Show me when I should give my all, please tell me what I need to do. Then as I bring the seed to You Lord, please allow my harvest to grow. I bring this gift with a cheerful heart Lord, just because I love You so.

God And Man

The God of all the universe spoke, and the entire world was made. He spread the planets out into space, and then all the season's He laid. Then He formed upon the earth, the object of His wonderful plan. He made a person in His very image, the creation He called man. He gave this man a helper, to share and subdue this place. They walked with God in the cool of the day, and spoke to Him face to face. Then God gave them a special task, and their obedience would surely decide. Yet they failed their test and lost their place, and from God they tried to hide. They now faced the curse of the judgment, and their glory began to die. God now banished them from His presence, and told them the reason why. Yet God still loved them very much, and He promised that He would redeem. That is why people have to work hard and struggle, to achieve each hope and dream. So then, one day God became a tiny baby, in the care of this fallen race. He came to remove all sin and death, to remove this evil disgrace. Once again, God walked with man in the person of His Only Son. Jesus Christ the Eternal God was anointed the Chosen one. Man was now so close to God, and yet so far away. Their hearts so hard and sin so evil, yet they missed this special day. While God became the sacrifice, to save the world He made. He brought the sin debt to the cross, so that the penalty could be paid. There upon a wooden cross, He was rejected of His own. He had no one to help or comfort Him; He went through it all alone. Soon darkness fell upon the land, where Jesus gave His all. His blood poured out to remove the curse, and the penalty of the fall. Now the ones who would come to the Father, to place faith in Jesus name. Could now receive eternal life, to be free from all their shame. One day soon, He will come again, to remove all evil and sin. There in the cool of that wonderful day, we will walk with God again.

UNAWARE

By going about our daily lives, we could all be caught unaware. When God calls out to those who are waiting, to meet Him in the air. Yet most of us are always searching, for a treasure we hope to find. So overwhelmed we miss His call, and find we are left behind. Oh, what pain to realize that this trouble will not disappear. For the world will be thrown into darkness, and our doubt has kept us here. The bible makes it very clear; we cannot have it all. You can worship money or worship God, but you who must make that call. God said the love of money is the root of every sin. Many never release it, but go after it again and again. For all that people seek today, are wealth, pleasure, and power. Yet when they discover they have been left behind, they will face a different hour. No more fun, no more games, and no more time to spare. All will go through a horrible time, and no one on earth will care. The time for saying maybe tomorrow, has finally arrived today. Now you must lay your life on the line, for God's grace has been taken away. It is time to prove just whom you serve, and heaven or hell will decide. You have been running from God for a very long time, but now you have no place to hide. The very next time He calls out to you, to ask you to receive His Son. May be the last time He calls your name and your decision will be done. So carefully weigh your destiny, choose the place where you would like to be. You can choose to accept God's wonderful Son or suffer for all eternity.

His Book

If your name is written in the Lamb's book of life there is something you should know. It is there because of your faith in Jesus, so in hell you will not go. For every name that is written there, will escape that terrible place. They have received the payment for all their sin and received God's loving grace. You see every person has value to God, a life He created with care. God will save each person in His book, every name that is written there. You can sign your name on a check you receive, or just write it in a book. That name will tell others just who you are, whenever they take a look. So you see your name is real special, a name that others know too. It may not carry a lot of weight, but it is one that was given to you. There is a name that is above every name; it is Jesus our Lord and King. One day everyone will bow before Him, the God above everything. On that day He will set on a throne and for your name, He will take a look. For only the family of the living God will have their name written in His book. The Lamb's book of life is just what it means. Every name there has been cleansed and made new. If you have asked Jesus to save your soul, then your name will be written there too.

LOOK AT ME NOW

As I was thinking back to when I was a child, I thought of those wonderful times I had. Just out climbing trees or maybe fishing in the river, but those times were seldom sad. We could buy candy for a single penny, and pop for just a dime. A movie for only fifty cents was free the second and third time. All our days were carefree ones, and there was nothing to do but play. It seemed this fun would last forever, and then we would begin another day. Then as I looked back to my younger years, I saw how the time had gone by. Gas was no longer thirty cents, and a gallon had gone sky high. I remember fishing all day long, where I seldom had to eat. When I fell down from being tackled in football, I just bounced back to my feet. Well as I am reminiscing about how it used to be, my thoughts return to the presence, and I see what has become of me. There is no more penny candy and the movies are not the same. Gasoline cost more then my car is worth, and every bill collector knows my name. I no longer have time for fishing, and to climb a tree would be quite an act. For my body bares the aches and pains, that can be felt in my lower back. It looks like I am getting older, for I cannot do those things I once did. Yet every time I think back to the past, I forget I am no longer a kid. Those were the days I cherished the most, things were wonderful and practically free. Yet I could not wait to get older and now just look at me. Yet being older is not all so bad I just hate to lose the time. Well I think I will go buy a bottle of pop, for a dollar fifty plus, one dime.

TEARS IN HIS EYES

I beheld the hand of wickedness and its envy scarred my soul. To see the world in such a terrible way, and watch it continue to grow. The lies all came in a different language, that only evil could comprehend. Still when they spoke of who was at fault, the truth they were quick to bend. I thought why do the people who continue to do evil always seem to get ahead. Then a voice that sounded like thunder spoke "their not living but walking dead." They may seem to you to have everything, and it may seem like they are so alive within. But the truth is they are empty and their spirit is dead with sin. Then an image of their judgment came, there were many before God's throne. All these souls stood bewildered, they were shameful and so alone. One by one, they all came before Him, and each time it was the same. As Jesus opened His book of life, He just could not find their name. While I stood there waiting for Him to accuse them, I was so shocked and so surprised. As I saw the expression of a broken heart and Jesus had tears in His eyes. I just could not believe the pain He was feeling, it was clearly not His desire. To see even one of these people He created, be condemned to the lake of fire. As I watched each one pass into eternity, I felt hurt and so filthy inside. I tried to be strong as I watched this judgment, but my pain I just could not hide. There was a time these people were winners, but now they are eternally lost. Sin had promised them many things, yet in the end look, what it cost. So I realized what I would have to do, when evil would seem to get its way. I would remind myself of the torment awaiting them, when they come to this judgment day. Then if it seems like they are getting ahead and my anger again starts to rise, I will think of my Saviors broken heart, and the tears that are in His eyes.

The Standard

He called me to the battleground with His weapon in my hand. The Word of God was my wisdom and knowledge, to high for mortal man. It was a call to active duty, a war with no retreat. One would defeat a thousand with a victory so complete. And still the enemy came in hard, with weapons so absurd. Yet all of God's children would be unbeaten, with the weapon being His word. One by one, the enemy fled no match for the Chosen one. As we spoke the name of Jesus, the enemy came undone. They slowly lost their foothold and in haste, they hit the street. Never stopping their angry rage that would soon be their defeat. Then all their accusations came, saying your soldiers do not fight fair. Yet all their lies were soon diminished, as God's light shined everywhere. Then their victor stood up to defend them, that old dragon in disguise. He had evil written all over him and a smirk with every lie. But the soldiers of the living God all stayed and held their ground. When the enemy came in like a flood, retreat could not be found. Why are you standing there waiting he said; are you not afraid of me? Yet the Spirit of God lifted a standard against him, and that old dragon turned to flee. Then the soldiers who stood there with the Lord, held His weapon above their head. For no one messes with the Word of God, there is power in all He has said. Every Christian has this weapon, which will cause the enemy to flee. God's Word is sharper then any sword when spoken righteously. The enemy may seem quite strong at times, but his only weapon is sin. Yet if you keep your eyes on Jesus, and speak His word, you will always win. Defeat the enemy with the blood of the Lamb, and the word of your testimony too. Then that devil will know that he is beaten, when he sees Jesus there with you.

Step Out On The Water

The water was splashing over the boat; the sails were being torn by the wind. As they tried to gain momentum, they found they were stuck within. Out in the middle where the storm blew strong and the wind splashed and whipped into their face. They prayed for an end to this raging storm, hoping for mercy and grace. Then in the distance they caught a glimpse, of what everyone thought was a ghost. Yet they stood in awe when they realized it was Jesus, God's Son the heavenly Host. Here was their Master walking on the water, conquering the wind and each wave. They knew they were safe from the pending disaster, for He had all the power to save. One of them said; if You are the Lord then bid me to come out on the sea. He said step out of the boat, and on to the water, just have faith and come here to Me. Slowly he started to move to his Master, but the wind started to blow once again. Jesus reached out and took a hold of his hand, just before he completely fell in. He said; why did you fear and lose your faith, you were already out on the sea. You have to know you will never be harmed, if you put your trust in Me. For all who believe and have faith in My words will master every storm that they see. Yet the winds and the waves will carry you under, if you take your eyes off of Me. If you have the faith to do whatever I say, you can conquer whatever you fear. All it will take is for you to believe in Me, just call out and I will be here.

They Have Taken It All

They have taken prayer out of the schools, and the bible is no longer curriculum they read. They want the Ten Commandments out of all public places, and they think they will succeed. They are trying to change the name of Christmas, so that Christ is out of the way. Still God will get the glory, for He owns every single day. Taking Jesus out of Christmas is like having gas without the car. It will not matter if you own a filling station; you will not get very far. You can take the bible out of your library but His Word will never die. God said His word would never pass away, no matter how much they try. You may not like our children praying, because it stops you from spreading your unbelief. Yet when the Creator judges you, you will never again know relief. You do not want the Ten Commandments, because they point to all your sin. But if you die without the Savior, no more heaven, you will not get in. So now, as touching Christmas for what this day is worth. It carries a special meaning, of our precious Savior's birth. It is not about your santa or the gifts you give to all, just switch a few of the letters around it spells satan who caused the fall. He wants the world to honor him, even if it is all for show. But celebrating this holiday your way, is like building frosty without the snow. You can rob and steal America's religion, but there is something you should know. This will always be a Christian nation, and our faith will always grow. So take your hands off our children and you will see that time will tell. When God has had enough of you, He will send you straight to hell. There you will not need the bible, but you will wish you had God's Word. Then every time you cry out in prayer, your screams will not be heard. Those Ten Commandments will no longer be important, to point you to your sin. For hell is the place where sinners go, a place you are already in. Still we will celebrate the birth of our Savior, and His word will never part. You will not be able to lie to our children, for they will have Jesus in their heart.

The Light Of God

From the moment, I entered this world in darkness, on the day when I entered in. All the roots that led from my family tree, were feeding from open sin. Yet somewhere in this darkness, I longed to see the light. Still how would I find the daylight, when around me was only night. I often looked up into the sky; I would ask if He were real. How can I be so empty inside, and who will take this pain I feel? Then one day when I finally had enough, and decided to quit the fight. I saw a glitter pierce the darkness, where I spotted a glorious light. So I pushed my way through the trouble and trials, to see if I could find my way. But darkness closed the door in my face, and tried to make me stay. A cry rose up from deep within me, and my voice came breaking through. Then I heard Him calling out to me, but I did not know what to do. Then came a mighty miracle, and in tears I began to pray. As I called on the name of Jesus, all the darkness went away. I walked into that glorious light, and His love began to shine. There I felt like I was forgiven, where my sins I left behind. Now each time I enter any darkness, the night begins to flee. I am filled with the light of Almighty God, and Jesus lives in me.

The Trinity

The Father, the Son, and the Holy Ghost, all three yet all the same. We are baptized in water, filled with His Spirit, by faith in Jesus name. We can heal the sick, cast out devils, and preach His word with power. We know that one day He is coming back, so we are waiting our midnight hour. Will you be ready to meet Him, should He call you to the air? Or are you planning on hanging around awhile, just because you do not care. Is the tribulation you're testing time that you think you must go through? Do you hear His Still Small Voice in your heart, as He tries to speak to you? Well there is something I need to tell you my brother, just before He takes us out. You have to put your faith in God, and remove each trace of doubt. Let His Holy Spirit lead you, He is the Comforter and your one true friend. The Spirit of our Lord and Savior, who will guide you to the end. All your help comes from the Father, through the Son and by the Holy Spirit. But will you know it is He who is speaking, and are you ready should you one day hear it? If you want to be sure of heaven, to one day see His face. He said that you must be born again, redeemed, and saved by grace. There is nothing to give, no price to pay, and no offering that will get you in. For Jesus shed His blood for everyone, to wash away our sin. So if you wear the name of Christian, then hold your head up high. For the Lord gave you a promise, that you will never have to die. The Father, Son and Holy Spirit are three and yet the same. I am glad I am called a Christian and I will proudly wear that name.

Seeds Of Faith

Give and it will be given like a seed that is planted deep. Your harvest time is coming soon, and what you have sown is what you will reap. If you have been planting seeds of faith, the Lord will meet your needs. Yet all the seeds that are evil ones will turn your harvest to weeds. God knows all the things we desire and He provides us tender care. But if God is the only one giving, tell me does that sound fair? Jesus came to save the lost, and His life is what He would give. Yet His sacrifice was more then money could buy, and far better then we could give. Though our God is up in heaven, and may seem so far away. He hears each word you speak to Him each time you kneel to pray. He said He loves a cheerful giver who never counts the cost; they give because they love Him, and want to reach the lost. So as you plant your seeds of faith, just remember what our God will do. He said think first of His kingdom above, and all things He will give to you.

Jesus Is Coming Soon

He walked out from the throne of God, and in reverence, they all bowed down. There were angels, elders and many creatures, which lay prostrate on the ground. The beauty of His holiness caused them all to stop and stare. For no one had seen such radiance, not on earth or anywhere. His voice sounded like a mighty trumpet, and had power in every word. They all cried holy holy holy, with every thing that they heard. The scars and the stripes He received on this earth, now stood as a reminder of His love. On earth, He was the Sacrificial Lamb, but He is the king of kings above. Wherever He would walk in heaven, they were ready at His command. Still He spoke with love and compassion, so that all could understand. The beauty of His continence reflected a servant's heart. Yet all who came to receive their reward were given a special part. He took time to stop for all of them, no matter how long it would take. Great joy would fill their spirit to the fullest, what happiness He would make. No darkness could enter His glory, for the light was too bright to bare. No matter how far away you were, His brilliance was everywhere. Every time He sat down on the throne, they would worship and praise His name. With the love and compassion He had for them, His mercy was always the same. So I will leave you this reminder, to get ready for the time is near. Jesus said soon He is coming back, and soon He will be here.

Proud To Be An American

I am proud to be an American in this land so wonderful and free. For God has kept us safe thus far, and shed His grace on thee. In this great land we live in, we can worship God above. We can lift our hands to praise Him, all because of His great love. Still it took a lot of bloodshed, from the ones who gave their all. They stood up to defend our country, so this nation would never fall. Our flag flies proudly in the sky with its red, white, and blue. It is there as a reminder, that God gave it all to you. This nation on earth has really been blessed, to feel this kind of grace. We have fought together in many wars, and still we hold our place. It was the dedication of the faithful people, who fought to keep us free. Who were not afraid to take up arms and fight for you and me. We Americans will always prevail, our togetherness is a must, to always remember why we are blessed. It is because "In God we trust". So we will never lose the battle as long as we are willing to stand. We will never lose our freedom if we are ready to defend our land. Yet this is not done with only weapons, or some leaders thought out plan. It is because we decided to turn from our sin, to our God's protective hand. Then He will bring the peace to us, He will come and heal our land. We must place our trust in God above, and then together we will stand.

THE GREAT LIE

Some people believe that human beings lived millions of years ago. But the only proof that they have of this, is the things they say they know. They say two planets collided in space and a tiny part fell down. It landed in a bit of water and began to swim around. Then as it lay there for millions of years, it grew hands, feet, and a tail. This they think is a scientific fact, and how could science fail? Then this object that lasted millions of years began to stand up straight. Now there you have it, a man with a tail, now I wonder where is his mate. They say this man was really hairy with a tail that hung down low. But keep in mind this is science, and they will swear to what they know. Now here we have a hairy beast, who from the water now breaths the air. Yet tell me why they quit coming out of the water, why did they choose to stay there? How did they lose all this hair they had, when it covered all of their skin. Did they also invent the barbershop, and one day just mosey in? Well they can really come up with good ones, to explain their cosmic birth. Then I stop and think for a moment, where did they get this earth? You also have the animals, from the large ones to the small. Did other planets explode over the earth and different particles fall? Some even say we are related to monkeys, and we resembled chimpanzees. Now that explains our love for bananas and our joy of climbing trees. So I wonder why we stay alone when we have nothing much to do. When we could go and visit our ancestors, who are locked inside the zoo. The devil keeps inventing ways to explain just how every man was made. To keep us from our Creator, and His holy plan He laid. They try to explain away creation yet they are left with only one flaw. God is the only Creator, and He created it all. He did not leave us guessing, and His word makes it crystal clear. Still some people would not listen, so God sent His Son down here. He could have let us believe those lies, and let this world be done. But He loved what He created, and so He sent His Only Son. Now people will always invent their ways to show how we were made. Yet all their ways are foolish, and over time, their lies will fade. So the next time someone comes around, saying this monkey lie is true. Just shove a banana in their mouth and please lock them in a zoo.

The Door To The Heart

The heart is like a hall of doors, and each door holds terrible dealings. Yet when you find what one has within, it may unlock many feelings. There is also an entrance, which leads to those doors, but it requires a special key. The Lord stands knocking at those doors, and waiting to set you free. Now He may get through the first door and even the next one too. But are you willing to open all of those doors, and let Him sup with you? He already knows the surprises inside, and He knows what you are trying to hide. Yet He wants to see if you really trust Him, or to see if you have lied. If you will open all those doors, and let the Savior in, He will pour His grace and mercy on you, and He will wash away your sin. For He wants to clean what is behind those doors, so He can purify your hearts. Yet He knows that you still hold the key and that is where your problem starts. Once you open all the doors, to let Him make you new. His Holy Spirit will enter in, and will come and live in you. So the next time you hear Him knocking, just remember His gift is free. Open that door and let Him in, and then give the Lord the key.

HELL IS A REAL PLACE

Hell is the place where the flame never dies, where the torment will never end. Hell is the place where all evil will go, and for all eternity they will spend. The devil will be cast to the lake of fire and will scream when he feels that flame. All the ones who choose to follow him will also feel the same. There are many ways of suffering, but fire will torment the most. I just cannot imagine why anyone, would want to be a part of that roast. For hell is the outcome of all the wicked souls, a place where they will not deny. This is the place called the second death, where they will suffer and never die. Hell is not just a hole in the ground or a place where the devil wears red. It is the place where you are separated from God, and from Him you are forever dead. Yes, the devil has something in common with hell, but it is not the place of his throne. You may even think you will have friends with you there, but like satan, you will be all alone. Hell was the place that was made for the devil, and the torment will not be a game. The devil knows he will one day be there, and his followers will be given the same. There is an escape to life over death, but it requires the master plan. Well Jesus is that Master who will help you to understand. Call on Him to save you; and do not join in satans lie. Do not let the devil lead you into hell, for there you will surely fry.

Hero's Of The Bible

The bible is filled with many heroes, not afraid to take a stand. They placed their trust in the God of all, and were guided by His hand. Ones like Noah who had faith to believe, to the saving of his own. By trusting, what the Lord said was coming; His mercy to him was shown. Abraham left his hometown while trusting God with out asking why. He was promised his seed would be great on earth, as many as the stars in the sky. How about Moses who started his mission, while still having a little doubt. Yet when he saw the greatness of God, he led the people out. Then there are prophets who were led by God, Like Elijah who heard all that He said. Even while standing up to those who came for him, by calling fire down on their head. There were so many heroes' who placed their lives on the line, to complete their earthly task. Their names will forever be written in heaven, where their memory will always last. Daniel braved the lions den for his faith in the One he believed. Many others were put to the test, with all the trials that they received. Like Sampson who beat the philistines, with a jawbone in his hand. Then we have Joshua who led Israel on, into the Promised Land. David destroyed the giant, who claimed to be the best, so he said. But a single stone with the power of God, and this enemy warrior was dead. The list of names goes on and on, too many to even write down. Will be forever in God's word, and their bravery will always be found. Let us not forget about Ruth and Esther, a daughter in law and a queen. Many women had faith to believe, yet some of them remained unseen. Truly, they were heroes of the faith and their names will forever live. For they trusted God as a way of life, and their all, they were willing to give. Now I would like to speak of One Hero, who greatly outweighs them all. Jesus is the greatest hero, who fulfilled His Father's call. He took this world so lost in sin, and came to die in our place. With no way out, we would surely die, while God extended His loving grace. He would not lose what He had created, even though sin made everyone dead. He removed the curse on a rugged cross, by dieing in our stead. So now, you know who the greatest hero is, for it is rather plain to me. That Jesus is the greatest hero, this world will ever see.

MY PROVIDER

Lord when I think of heaven, oh the glory of that place. It takes me back to years ago when I first received Your grace. With all the people, I have preached to, in the glory of Your name. I often wonder how they are doing and if the joy they had, is the same. The cares of this life can wear us down, and cause our faith to slide. So we need to keep our eyes on You, with your Spirit as our guide. Because there is trouble on every side, that just will not leave us alone. In times like these when we are hurting the most, we wish You would bring us home. There are people we meet who say they have faith, yet stumble, and take a fall. Some will get up and start again, while others lose it all. Yet we feel their tears inside our soul, like bleeding with no end. While we pray for a revival, or even a refreshing wind. We watch the ones who say they are followers, reward evil with the same. Even though they know that they are wrong, they do it in Your name. Lord I know that You have plans for us but what are we to do. When we take the burdens all to ourselves, instead of bringing them all to You. Some believers say they do not worry, yet their fear shows that this is not true. When their bills come in, and the car breaks down, or their mortgage payment is due. Still if this is not enough to handle, there is no money for them to try. They say they have faith to always believe, but forget who is their supply. So help me Lord to see my blessings, and all those things that I have got. Show me Lord How to trust in You, increase my faith a lot. Remove the tears I have in my heart, and those things, which I have been through. Teach me how to overcome, so I can one day live with You. Show me how to be patient as I struggle through another day. Then I will bring my burdens to You, each time I kneel and pray. Strengthen me when I am weak, and supply when I am in need. Help me plant Your faith in others, and then You supply the seed. Then if I stumble along the way, for some reason I cannot understand. Reach to the bottom of all of my suffering Lord, and take me by the hand. Stand me up on solid ground, where I know I will never fall. For Lord you are my Provider, and in You I have it all.

The Body Of Christ

The church is called the body of Christ it has many members too. We are called the brethren of the Lord, and we all have work to do. Some are called to the ministry, others to the missionary field. But all of His children are called for a purpose; they all are born again and sealed. Some are set aside for teaching, and some will heal the same. Yet no one can claim the glory, for it is done in Jesus name. Now you may have a word for others, just be ready to give your all. No matter what your ministry may be, it is important to answer God's call. Now you could speak to millions of souls, or preach to only one. Yet your reward is being stored up in heaven, when all your work is done. All that you do in the name of Jesus, no matter how small it may appear. Is great in the kingdom of heaven, for the Lord is always here. Every born again believer young or old the same. They are called to this great commission, to preach salvation in Jesus name. God is the One who searches our hearts, and distributes these gifts to His own. Your rewards will be given for what you have accomplished, with all of the seeds you have sown. So the very next time you do a work for the Lord, just remember that work will soon grow. God does not want for even one soul to parish, and so you could be there for only that soul. Preach in the name of Jesus, as an ambassador is sent to do. And always keep in mind the reason you preach, because Jesus is counting on you.

A Smile

A smile is like a special tool that is used in many ways. Sometimes it fixes what is broke, and the result is one that stays. You see when someone starts to smile, and others begin to see. It may cause a chain reaction that can end up with two or three. So if someone makes you angry and violence has crossed your mind. Just start to smile it can ease the tension, try it, and see what you find. People try to read our looks, to see what we have inside. But when you smile, they are not sure, because joy is hard to hide. While a smile can be with you all your life, even when you are laid to rest. If your life was in Christ Jesus, your smile will be the best. So when the world has gotten you down, and you do not know what to do. Just place a smile upon your face, and maybe they will too.

The Blood Of Jesus

In the darkest night with a star filled sky, the Savior knelt to pray. For no one in this world had His understanding but still He chose to stay. He knew the reason that He was sent and He knew what He came to do. He was ready to die a cruel death and remove all our punishment too. But there was more that He would accomplish all the things we could not see. We were bound by a curse of sin and death, and He came to set us free. A light would shine in this darkened world, the day that Jesus came. Yet some loved the darkness more then the light, so they chose to remain the same. Still Jesus would offer His forgiveness, to even those who caused His pain. His blood would flow to those that believed, like drops of cleansing rain. When you feel like you are all alone, with the darkness all around. Just ask the Lord to come into your heart, and salvation will be found. Turn to Him and repent of your sins, and the Lord will understand. Because now is the day of salvation, for heaven is at hand. Jesus will wash away your sin; He will come and make you whole. Then you will know you are born again, by His blood you will be whiter then snow.

City Of David

Holy Zion the city of God, the land of the Holy One. A place where God will live with His people, with Jesus Christ His Son. His Holy temple has been started, with the foundation being laid. A corner stone was put in place the entire price was paid. All the pillars were set in rolls, and His name is above the door. With streets and sidewalks clear as crystal, and gold laid as a floor. Bless the land where God will dwell, no evil will ever get in. for Jesus the Son has given His blood, to wash away all sin. This city that God is building will one day be complete. All the enemy's of our Lord will be crushed beneath His feet. So bless this land called Zion, a city where David was blessed. For we are His temple that He is building and we will one day enter His rest. Then we will see a special day, when we enter that holy place. We will take the hand of our Savior, for we are saved by His wonderful grace. That is why we wait for a city, one not made with our hands. God knows we are His children and are part of His holy plans. One day this city will descend from the heavens, a New Jerusalem where our God will dwell. The believers will spend eternity with Jesus, and will never taste of hell.

Last Seven Year's

One day all religion will be outlawed, and to have a weapon will be a crime. The earth will have only one leader, who will promise true peace for a time. Yet when they all cry peace and safety, their trouble will begin. For in this world of darkness, man will be filled with all kinds of sin. The time will come when men will be afraid, for what is coming on this earth. They will suffer at the hands of evil, who will mock their very birth. With a worldwide shortage of food and water, survival will depend on their skill. They will have to hide from this evil tyrant, who is always out for the kill. He will cause the world to receive his mark, or the number of his name. But when the people receive his image, like him they will be the same. This entire world will plunge into darkness, a time where no person will be free. There will never be another time like this that anyone will ever see. Death will become a common thing, with no rules or law to keep. Many will live like hardened criminals, who are too afraid to sleep. You will not be able to buy from the store, unless you wear his mark. Yet those who decide to hide away will only come out after dark. This is the time when the wrath of God, will be poured out on sinful man. All who decide to reject His Son will be in this end time plan. The Lord will give them what they desire, to be free from His holy word. Then they will see that it is too late, for the preaching that they once heard. They will curse the pain that they all feel, and will wish that they could die. Yet death will flee and they will suffer, and they know the reason why. The tribulation is coming soon and then you will have to decide. Do you want to live forever with Jesus, or stay down here and hide? Call on the Lord to save your soul, and please do not hesitate. For when the Christians leave this planet, your chance may be too late.

Resurrection Joy

With a flash of lightning, and the explosion of thunder, the Son of God now dead. Fallen hopes and uncertain dreams, their joy now lost instead. As they took His body down from the cross, and washed His blood away. They placed Him in a borrowed tomb, to prepare for the Sabbath day. Their broken hearts now in dismay, and wondering what should now be done. Would they return to what they did before, they met God's Holy Son? Some of them hid away in fear and others in disbelief. Trying to decide what they should do, as now their hearts felt grief. They went to prepare His body, as the custom was for the dead. Taking their spices and what was needed, but they forgot what the Lord had said. As these women all went down to the tomb, the stone was rolled away. An angel was seated on the stone and they were amazed at what they heard him say. Why do you seek the living, here among the dead? He is not here He is risen, don't you remember what He had said? They ran and told His disciples, the things they heard the angel say. Two of them took off for the tomb, running all the way. But the body of Jesus was not there, just the wrappings that He had worn. All of them were neatly folded and not one of them were torn. Mary stayed there at the tomb weeping and looking in, this was the one who was delivered from bondage, and forgiven of all her sin. Then she was startled by someone behind her, it was Jesus her Master and King. She finally realized that it was the Lord, and her soul began to sing. Tell My friends that I have risen, and shortly they will see. Then He came and showed Himself to all of them, and their doubt began to flee. They knew that He would always be with them, to supply what they would need. For they finally realized that the Lord had risen, the Lord has risen indeed.

It Was Him

He called the world into existence, and was there when man disobeyed. He was the one who designed the galaxy, before anything was made. He was there when Noah built the ark, and it was Him who caused the rain to fall. He was there when man began to fill the earth; He was there to see it all. It was Him who led Israel out of Egypt, and it was Him who gave them their land. It was Him who promised to supply their need, as He held them in His hand. It was Him who sent them prophets that would show them what to do. It was Him who brought them out of their bondage, all the trouble that they went thru. It was Him who showed us we were sinners, by giving us His word. It was Him who called us out of darkness, the Still Small Voice we heard. It was Him who said we were guilty, and the payment for sin was death. It was Him who breathed His life into us, and Him who could remove that breath. It was Him who came to show us the way, and it was Him who caused me to cry. For it was I who was the guilty one, but it was Him who chose to die. Then He covered me in His blood, and He washed away my sin. So that one day when He calls me to heaven, it will be Him who lets me in.

WONDERFUL HOLY SPIRIT

Oh, precious Holy Spirit come and fill this empty soul. Teach me how to live my life, fill me until I am full. Give your gift of speaking in tongues, and change my heart within. Let me feel that oil of joy, and help me not to sin. Give me the words that I should speak, and a vision for the lost. Help me to see all that Jesus has purchased, let me never forget the cost. Use my hands for more then just praying, and lead someone into my path. So that I can warn them to escape the fire, to deliver them from the coming wrath. Make me a vessel fit for the Master; let my body be the temple where You dwell. Help me my Lord to warn the lost, about the terrible pit of hell. I love you Holy Spirit, please pour Your oil on me. Open my spiritual eyes my Lord then please come and help me to see. Jesus I praise You for Your wonderful love and the joy that You placed in my soul. Please come and live inside my heart and Lord please do not ever go. Wash me, cleanse me, and change me my Lord, so I will never be the same. Then seal me forever my Lord, by the power of Your name. Holy Spirit lead me, through this life that I now live. Help me to walk by faith alone, with every blessing that You give. Walk with me Lord each and every day, and my Lord please stay close to my side. For You are the One who will lead me home, my Comforter, and my Guide.

The Spoken Word Became Living

It blossomed in a moment and the beauty reflected its worth. At first His word was spoken, and behold the planet earth. Then in a state of sheer design, came a plan that could not die. Yet the man and woman made a fatal choice, to believe an evil lie. The entire world would be affected, and nothing would be the same. They were stripped of all their dignity, to wear another's name. The hand of the Master Designer, knew just what, would soon take place. He knew that mankind would need a Savior, to redeem the human race. It seemed that time had now stood still, and their hopes would slowly fade. Through the muck and mire of daily life, the creation now would wade. Forever repeating the same mistakes, and even coming up with new. No one had an answer, to what they all would do. Yet the Lamb of God would come face to face, with death, hell and the grave. All of mankind would be redeemed, by the One who had the power to save. The pit of hell shook violently, as if to see this loss. The demons all screamed crucify, as He was nailed to the cross. There He was hanging, between heaven and earth, as His final word was said. In a commanding voice, He said; "IT IS FINISHED" and the Lamb of God was dead. The earth was shaken and the thunder roared, as the Veil in the temple tore in two. Hell was shaken so violently, that devil knew he was through. Three days had passed and when all was forgotten, they were reminded of the words He said. For now, His promise had been fulfilled as He rose up from the dead. Once again, on a shining morning, the beauty reflected His worth. For God had proved His Word was true, of how He would save the earth. All creation stood in awe, at this miracle the Lord had done. He took the place of the guilty, by giving to us His Son. The curse of the law of sin and death, He then nailed to that tree. So that nothing would separate us from the love God, which He had for you and me.

CROSS ROAD

Death is the doorway, which leads to the eternal, a departure from this physical realm. Those who are saved have no limits or boundaries, nothing to overwhelm. Time as we know it is not the same, for to die will not happen again. Those who were lost will be tormented and imprisoned, for no payment was made for their sin. Both will live for all of eternity, but only one will know they are free. For all of their sins were nailed to the cross, they were redeemed at Calvary. Jesus Christ the Son of God paid the price when He died in our stead. Beaten and bleeding He hung on that cross, and He suffered until He was dead. There at the crossroad of death and the grave, a choice was laid in the path. Those who rejected this way to the Father would one day feel His wrath. But all who would call on the Savior of life, were forgiven, and sealed and freed. There was nothing more they would have to do; He was everything they would need. Two doors were opened leading to death or life, a choice that no man could hide. In death, you would only see suffering, but life had Jesus inside. He gave blessings and freedoms, and eternal life, but the choice you would have to make. Your decision will then be eternal, so be sure of the one you take. You can take heaven or hell whatever the choice this decision belongs to you. But once you leave the land of the living, your chance to choose is through. Now you are at the cross road, where you have to decide your eternal place. You can choose to live with Jesus forever, or suffer in hell and disgrace.

God's Love For Us

You may deliver your entire tithe, down to the very cent. You may even have given your offerings, not knowing where they went. You might not miss a day of church, where you lift your hands and sing. But if you neglected the love of God, your gifts did not mean a thing. God is not impressed with money, and He does not need a song. All He requires is your righteous living, so stop doing what is wrong. You lift your hands as if you know Him, and then hate your brother too. You find you cannot forgive them, but you think that God forgives you. You like it when all the church sees you, how holy you can be. But look inside at the real you that only God can see. Money will not deliver you; no wealth will make you strong. You may think that God is forgetting, all the things that you are doing wrong. It is true you have been a giver, and no person can deny. Yet if you say you have done it for God, be careful not to lie. You cannot hate your brother and give to God your best. For though you have kept the first part, you have neglected all the rest. God said to love your neighbor, regardless of what it cost. It does not matter what you have to give, to try to save the lost. Our lights must always brightly shine, so that the entire world can see. That Jesus paid the highest price, salvation was not free. He did not do it to please Himself, or the rewards that waited above. He did it because He wanted us to know His Father's love. This gift was not in money, but it cost Him all He had. So that one day we could join His family, and call His Father dad. You may not know how much He loves you, for those tears were not shed in vain. If they were to fall upon the earth, you could never stop that rain. So when you think you have given plenty and your righteous deeds will do. Just remember God out gave us all, and did it because He loves you. Do not lift your hands and pretend to know

Him, if you do not show your brother love. For even if you give all the wealth that you have, it is not seen above. You see God made you and me the same, and we are His very best. Some of us may live in poverty, while others may be blest. It does not mean He loves someone more, just because they have a lot. For you are very special to Him no matter what you have got. So the next time you are feeling righteous, and you decide to make a show. When your right hand is getting ready to give, do not allow your left hand to know. Then God may see your giving and reward you from above. Just remember when you do the first; do not forget to give His love.

FALLING AWAY

Father when I see my Christian brothers began to fall from grace. I feel the pain inside my heart, to see them drop out of the race. It seems as though they have given up and began to believe a lie. Blinded to where their sin will lead them, forgetting why Your Son had to die. I know that we are in Your hands, and that You are the Judge of our soul. Still we feel sorry for those who walk away, with nowhere left to go. Lord, I remember reading Your word, about when Peter denied You that night. After You rose up from the dead, You forgave and brought him back to Your light. Yet what about those who turn their backs, and simply walk away? Will they be restored or forever condemned; will they still have a chance to pray? Father please give us wisdom, and help us until You call us home. Teach us to keep our eyes on You, never leave us on our own. Jesus please keep us in Your sight, and protect us from that evil lie. So that we can spend eternity with You, so we will never have to die. Lord I will keep on praying for my brothers, who may have lost their way. That they may see how sin is destroying them, and turn back to You today. Help them Lord to see the truth, that hell is open wide. They that wish to enter that place will have their chance inside.

THE LITTLE CHURCH

In a little church so long ago, a sinner would kneel and pray. As the choir, all sang just as I am, to the front he would make his way. All of these saints, some now gone home, would rejoice in his delight. For here another soul was saved, and brought to God that night. Many years have come and gone, but that little church still stands. For God has been there so many times, He keeps them in His hands. At this altar, they would kneel and pray, while their tears of repentance would fall. The pastor would lay his hands on their heads, as the Spirit would enter them all. They still sing songs while salvation takes place, and rejoicing can still be heard. And every time as they have church, you will always hear God's word. The entire bible is preached here, where many lost souls are saved. Sins are being forgiven, with freedom to those enslaved. Still they all come just as they are, to worship in this place. They sing the songs of long ago, of His wonderful amazing grace. In a quiet town in a little church, a son and a daughter will pray. Children of one, who was lost one day, are now ready to change their way. They walk down to the altar with people singing, as they come and kneel down. The choir sings a new song, of how another sinner was found. A lasting faith and the love of the Savior, with these believers to lead the way. A family that was saved in this little church are forever with Jesus today.

Jim, Vikki, Stella, Betty, Rick, and Gloria

A Day With The Lord

How would you feel if Jesus decided to spend a day with you? Would
that make you change your attitude, or those things you normally do?
How about all those feelings you have, like bitterness, anger and strife.
Will He see in you a servant's heart, when He looks into your life? He
may just want to go shopping with you, to see how your day will start.
Oh but those words coming out of your mouth, as someone bangs into
your cart. Later He may set down at your table, to see how you keep
your books. He may wonder why you cheat on your taxes, and call
other people crooks. What if He asks you to loan Him your new car,
just to see what you will say. What will you do if He gives back the
keys, and says to give this car away? What about your religious living,
is your home life and church life the same? Or will He see that you are
different, and playing a Christian game? What if He should ask if He
could live with you, would it cause you to change your plans? Or would
you welcome Him into your home, because your life is in His hands.
What if you did not know it was Jesus; would you still treat Him like
your friend? Or would you send Him out into the cold, because your
rules you could not bend? If a man does not work he should not eat,
this has been your favorite verse. If he is not rich, then he is not like you,
but walking in a curse. So you send this stranger on his way, and you
make your judgment clear. Even if God had called him to you, it is as
if you did not hear. But what if this visitor was Jesus, who wanted to
see what you would do? What if you left Him naked, cold, and hungry,
what then would He think of you? I know you believe you would not
have to worry, just to walk with the Lord for one day. But the truth is
He wants to live in you, to enter your heart and stay. Yet a house that
has no master, or a lamp without its light. Would be like a building full

of clutter, or eyes that have no sight. Jesus wants to set you free, so why not come and give Him a try. He said that He would come and live in you, and you know He cannot lie. So the next time some one comes to you, just be careful what you say. That person just may be Jesus, who has come to spend the day.

Just Like Me

One day as I sat there wondering, about all the suffering that I see. All the battered children and broken lives, why can't they be set free? I saw people held in bondage, with nowhere they could turn. Continuing in this life of pain, all because they do not learn. They struggle through another day just hoping for the best. Throwing out all the good things in life, while keeping all the rest. How long will they keep repeating this cycle, of playing the same old song? When will they finally realize, this pain does not belong. I saw an alcoholic passed out, with a bottle of whiskey by his bed. I thought who would tell his children when their daddy is found dead. I saw a needle shoved into an arm, to feed this addicts high. Yet how do you dry the mother's eyes, when she sees her baby die? How about all the lonely souls, who keep their hurt inside? With a heart that never loved another and the tears, they always hide. I started to wipe my tear stained eyes, just wondering where to begin. Thinking about all those souls that were lost, those who covered their lives with sin. Here are people who suffer on earth, who lived their life in pain. Now they may choose to die without Jesus, this thought was so insane. One by one, they would pay the price, and then feel that eternal flame. All because they were lost in sin and never called His name. Then I said let go of your pain, let the Lord remove your sin. Then when you leave this life on earth, you will not have to suffer again. Then as I turned to look at a sinner, I was amazed at what I could finally see. Every person that I passed that day, were sinners just like me.

What About God

I wonder what God was feeling, when Adam and Eve began to hide? When He entered the garden on that dreadful day, I wonder what He was feeling inside. Does He hurt in His heart when He sees us fail; are there tears in His eyes when we sin? Does it get Him excited when we say we are sorry, and does He hurt when we fail again? I often wonder about our Awesome God, and I wonder what He feels in His heart. He watches His children fall into sin, and still His love does not part. I wonder about how He is feeling, because I know how I would feel. I do not think that I could handle it, seeing my children lie and steal. I know what I would be thinking, as I held them in my hand. My hurt would turn to anger, and I would make them understand. But God is always patient and He is ready to forgive. Our lives are held in His awesome hands, and He allows us all to live. Now if He can let His Son die for me, and suffer on an old rugged cross. Then we can never know what He was feeling, we have never felt such loss. Well I may not know what God feels inside, but there is one thing that I do know. He loves His children with all of His heart, and He will always love us so. So when your heart is broken and you are feeling hurt inside. Remember how much God loved you, with a love He did not hide. Then when you wonder if anyone cares, and you feel your out on a limb. Stop for one minute and think how God feels, then ask yourself, What About Him.

You Do Not, So You Get Not

You do not see the miracle, of the food He gave that day. Five thousand fed plus many leftovers, from a gift someone gave away. You do not see all the blessings each day that often pass you by. So you do not receive your harvest, and you continue to ask God why. So many things He sends your way, yet you do not have eyes to see. Many of these blessings are still coming, but still you just let them be. You miss the stilling of your storm, with out the power of His Word. You miss the things that God has spoken, things no man has heard. You miss the love of His gentle touch, which is given by His hand. Sometimes He speaks in a Still Small Voice, but you just do not understand. You miss the chance to be filled with the joy, of walking with Him everyday. Because you have your own set of rules, while His get in your way. You miss the gift of healing, because you want it all alone. You miss the fact that He is the healer, and will always heal His own. Now if this sounds just like you my friend, there is something you should do. Get on your knees and ask the Lord, to come in and empower you. Ask Him to fill you with His Spirit, and to open your spiritual eyes. Tell that devil to hit the road, and stop believing his evil lies. Then put God's word into your heart and mouth, and walk as if you own the day. Tell the world that Jesus has risen and that He is the only way. Then watch for all His blessings, not the way you used to do. Yet keep your eyes on the great God above, knowing Jesus lives in you. Remember it is not by what you do, for it is He who does it all. Just keep in mind Who stands behind you, and will never let you fall. Just ask any thing according to His word, and He will supply all you will need. Then as your blessings turn into your harvest, remember He supplies the seed.

COMMISSIONED

We are part of a great commission, to go and preach to the lost. Yet our preaching must be to every person, regardless of the cost. He said preach in season and out of season, for there will surly come a day. When the world will be so evil, not desiring what you say. Now is the day of salvation, but this time is slipping away. When they will resist the word that is spoken, and surely miss that day. But we should never give up on even one, as long as we have a chance to try. For with God all things are possible, and the bible does not lie. He said the harvest is truly plentiful, but the laborers are so few. That is why He said to go, and He will be right there with you. Are we sure that they are ready to receive, that is something only God will know. All that matters is that we obey His word, for all He said was go. If you believe He loves you, then be a servant in His sight. Then go into the entire world, and preach with all your might. You may have tribulation, but remember He had the same. Just preach His word with power and might, and preach in Jesus name. Then if one soul believes what you are saying, and is saved by what is heard. Then God will receive the glory so go, and preach His word.

Meet Me On The Other Side

Sometimes in life, we see loved ones or friends, who have finished their earthly stay. They are entering into a new beginning, to start a brand new day. We go to them and pray for deliverance, praying that maybe God will heal. But deep inside where the tears we hide, we are concerned of how we will feel. We love and know we will miss them, and this loss will be hard to bare. Deep in our soul, we know they are ready, for Jesus will meet them there. So we cry and we tell them we love them, and we will see them on the other side. We try to be strong for the others, but our feelings are just to hard to hide. Then when we are alone all by ourselves, the pain begins to sting. As tears begin to fill our eyes, we thank our God, for the comfort He will bring. As you look into the face of the one who is leaving, you wonder if life is fair. You, thank God, they are saved and you say your goodbyes placing them in our Father's care. Here is a Father who watched His Son die, He has a heart that can feel hurting too. He knows every time that we feel our loss, and He will always be there for you. So as our loved ones go home to be with the Lord, let us remember they are in His great care. One day soon we will see them again, when our wonderful Lord calls us all there.

Worship At Your Feet

My Holy Father in heaven I come to praise Your name. No matter how much I come before You, Your love is always the same. I want to lift my hands to You, to worship without doubt. Please search my heart for any evil and Lord please take it out. Wash me in Your cleansing blood, and forgive me of all my sin. For one day when I leave this earth, I want to live again. Where I can come into Your throne room, and worship there anew. Where angels all sing songs of praise, as they bow and worship You. I want to see You face to face, to feel Your wonderful love. Please help me here to worship You, as I will in heaven above. Change my heart to a fleshly one and make my whole life new. Then lead me to a place of joy, where I will always honor You. Let my prayers come up before You, as sweet incense before Your throne. Fill me with Your Holy Spirit so I will never be alone. I love You Lord with all my heart no other deserves my praise. You are my Lord and Savior, and I will worship You all my days. Then one day when I come to heaven, I will fall down at Your feet. All the glory will go to You Lord and my joy will be complete. There may be tears falling from my eyes, but I know You will understand. For I was created for Your purpose, and a part of Your master plan. So when I fall down at Your feet, all my worship will be true. For as I look into Your face, I will say Lord "I Love You."

Why Do I Believe

You want to know the reason I believe in God, I am glad you ask me why. Look at the birds that have no worry, as they fly so very high. Then you have the flowers of the fields, with their beauty so wonderful indeed. Yet each unlike the other, and all from a tiny seed. The sky above may be blue all day, but is it the same at night? Or does it lose its luster, when it is taken from the light. Then I think of the sun in the sky, burning bright for years no doubt. For thousands of years it just keeps on burning, and still it does not go out. Then I watch the clouds in the sky, so high above the ground. They float on by us all the time, yet none of them fall down. Then we have the air we breathe, from where does this gentle wind flow? We feel the wind and the breeze it brings, but do we really know? Yet that is not the only reason I believe, so let me take you to the start. To a long time ago when I was alone and empty, and Jesus came into my heart. Never before in my whole life, have I felt the way I feel. When His wonderful love came over me, then I knew that He was real. That day I confessed Him with my mouth, and believed inside my heart. He filled me with His Spirit, and promised He would never part. So if you are wondering why I believe, and if you wonder if the bible is true. Just confess Him with your mouth, and ask Him into your heart. Then you will believe in God too.

THE LITTLE TREE

One day a person planted some trees, and lined them in a row. Then over the years the trees he planted, slowly began to grow. Yet in this row was a smaller tree that just could not seem to sprout. While the other ones were getting taller, this little tree just grew out. All the trees grew way up high, but the little one stayed low. Standing next to these massive trees, he knew he would have to go. The little tree tried everything; he lifted his branches up high. Still he only stretched out a little, and soon began to sigh. The other trees were very proud they ignored the smaller tree. They told him you will amount to nothing, and a twig is all you will be. But over the years, this tiny tree began to grow and grow. While the other trees just mocked him, saying a shrub belongs down low. And then one day the call came out, one of you will be taken down. You will be honored in a special way, no greater will be found. All the trees were excited, to hear that one would be this prize. Yet when the day came to choose the tree, they could not believe their eyes. The woodsman came to pick a tree, but the bigger ones were too tall. One by one, they checked them over, but quickly passed them all. Then they came to the little tree, and decided it would do. Little tree they said to him, the honor goes to you. All the other trees just watched, as his splendor showed around. The woodsmen took their axes out, and cut him to the ground. The taller trees began to laugh, they were glad to see his loss. Yet on a hill called Calvary, they saw it fashioned into a cross. The little tree became a symbol of what anything can be, for God came down and saved the world by dieing on a tree.

The Only Way

They followed Him from town to town, wherever He would go. Some were saved and some confused, for He spoke words no man could know. He often spoke of leaving, but they could not understand. How could He be the Son of God, and still be Fully Man. So they watched to see if He made a mistake, and they used their knowledge of the law. But none could trick the very One, who was there to create it all. He stopped to heal many people, and He fed their hungry soul. He spoke to them in terms they knew, while the broken He made whole. Still they sought a sign from heaven, to confirm His sovereign right. They kept on walking in the darkness, ignoring His holy light. Some would see the miracles done, and believe without a doubt. While others held to their traditions that left them no way out. But no one could see the things He saw, how He would die upon a cross one day. That by His death and by His blood, all sin would be taken away. They watched to see Him falsely accused, and saw Him beaten in their sight. Yet no one stood in His defense, or said this was not right. There on that hill in all their sight, where many criminals had died. They placed a cross between two thieves, and God's Son they crucified. There hung the hope of every soul, who would spill His blood for them all. To remove the curse of sin and death, and to redeem them from the fall. They walked with Him, and talked with Him, and they saw Him die that day. Yet that was what He came to do, to show them all the way. With His hands stretched out and His heart full of love, the Saviors work was done. Now the way to the Father in heaven, was through Jesus Christ His Son.

THE FATHER WAIT'S

The sun began to rise in the sky, in the early summer morn. As two sons would awake to tend the fields, there father now too old and worn. While the youngest thinking about the city, a carefree life indeed. With what he would get with his inheritance, he had all that he would need. But to wait seemed like a lifetime, as each day was being spent. So he came to his father and asked for his share, he took what was his and went. When he finally arrived to this crowded city, he sort of felt out of place. Yet he saw the cares and the pleasures around him, and a smile came on his face. He began to spend his living, on wine, woman, and song. Never stopping to realize, that this way of living was wrong. Deep into the shadows of darkness, with every type of sin. He played the game that they all were playing, and he quickly fit right in. He spent until he was nearly broke, as he partied every night. While at home, his father was worrying and praying, into the morning light. Alone and broke he came to himself, and realized what he had done. For even his father's servants, ate better then this wicked son. So he decided to go back to his father's home, he was feeling like a miserable wreck. Yet when his father saw him from a distance, he came running and hugged his neck. Now think of how our Father feels about us, who have strayed out on our own. He has waited for us to realize our faults, to turn around and come back home. He never stops searching, for those who are lost, even those who are led astray. Yet He keeps on watching from a distance, for us to return one day. So when you finally come to yourself, and realize what you put yourself through. Just remember the Father wants you to come home, He is watching and waiting for you.

IN HIS IMAGE

Why did God create us different, that is what many would like to know? He could have made us all the same, when the world began to grow. Yet He chose to create us in His image, with languages for every land. Where time would be the solution, by dividing every man. Every person on this earth is different, in a very special way. They were created for a special purpose, to be revealed to them some day. There are kings and queens, rich and poor, even children in His plan. Yet His grand design was not real easy for some to understand. Some people question why they were made, and even dread that they were born. But every soul here on this earth, fills a void in a heart that is torn. Some are poor in earthly treasure, yet rich in spiritual love. Some are good while others are bad, with no hope for heaven above. Still in our lonely hours when all our hope was lost, God could see what He had made and would save at any cost. You may not feel like He cares for you, while you may be lost in sin. Yet God has made a way for you to join Him once again. So you see you have the God of all, who loves you for who you are. He made you for a wonderful purpose, just like a shining star. To Him we are all made the same and in riches, we have great worth. He knew you before your parents, and even before your birth. So remember you are very special, no matter what others may say. God wants you to spend eternity with Him that is why Jesus made a way. Call upon the name of the Lord, and be glad what He made of you. For He created us a lot like Him, and we are in His image too.

Banished

One day I was thinking about the souls that were lost, and wondering about their fate. These were banished to a fiery lake, their forgiveness now too late. Stuck inside this prison of pain, with fire, smoke, and steam. And with agony and suffering so terrible, it was to difficult to even scream. Biting down on their tongues in pain, and gnashing down on their teeth. As another one enters, they fall on top pushing the others way down beneath. There is no more fun and no more enjoyment, and there is no one to quench this fire. As they try to move away from the others, the flame grows higher and higher. Fire and brimstone without any liquid, not a drop to quench any thirst. Heat that never cools or goes out, so hot you feel you will burst. But while you have been there a thousand years, your forever has only just begun. For you gave up your chance, to be with God in heaven, by rejecting Jesus His Son. Your flesh will dissolve a million times, but no one can hear you cry. Over and over, the pain will continue, but you will never die. Then after His judgment day is over, and you are sent to this horrible place. You will be banished to suffer in hell forever, and never again see His face. This lake of fire is a real place, but this suffering does not have to be. All you have to do is ask Jesus to save you, before your cast to this fiery sea. If you leave this earth without the Lord, your suffering will never be done. For there is only One person who can save your soul, and Jesus is that One.

MARRIAGE

Marriage is a sacred contract, that ties the knot of love. And if those vows were true that you both made, they will be blest by God above. For this reason, a man will leave his parents, and be joined unto a wife. The two of them will then become one, and be together the rest of their life. That day that you were married, it was more then just the two. For marriage is a Holy covenant, and God joined in it too. Jesus came and watched the wedding, and heard those words you spoke. For God does not hold it lightly, for to him it is no joke. Your marriage can be a real blessing, where two souls can be complete. Where God can bless that marriage and the pleasure can be so sweet. Yet a marriage requires the both of you, so that the other can never fall. Then if the burden of life gets to heavy, then God will take it all. But you have to remember that it requires faith, and then no one can pull you apart. For when God sees this special marriage, He will come and bless your heart. You have to work on it every day, and keep God in your marriage too. For what He has brought together, nothing on earth can undue. So join in a special wedlock, where you will stay with the one you love. Then God will always watch over your marriage, from the portals of heaven above.

THANKSGIVING

Thanksgiving is a special time, for friends and family to share. To remind ourselves of all our blessings and to be thankful for our Father's care. We may not have all the things we would like, and sometimes we may wonder why? Yet God will surely meet our needs, for He is our supply. Some may not give Him the glory, because their god is not the same. They do not count their blessings, but look for others to blame. Many people in this world go hungry, still God tends to every need. That is why He loves a cheerful giver, for holding back is greed. So count your blessings every day, and be there to lend a helping hand. Try to show someone that they are blessed, even if they do not understand. Remember to count all the blessings you have, as you set down at your table to eat. If you are carrying a heavy burden, then lay it at Jesus feet. Cast all your care upon the Lord, for He knows what you are going through. Then remember the blessing, that brings thanksgiving, it is Jesus living in you. This is the blessing God has chosen over all, His Son that knows no greed. He will surely come and give His blessing, to every one who is in need. So count your blessings on this Thanksgiving Day, and remember that none are small. God will pour them on those who ask, just because He loves us all.

Paid In Full

Whom do you want me to release to you, this one called Jesus the King of the Jews? No, they cried release Barabas and Pilate cringed at this horrible news. He did not want to let this murderer go, but the people kept on shouting their plea. So this innocent man would be put to death, and the guilty one would go free. There standing on the pavement, as this murderer was let go. His eyes locked on the innocent one, this person he did not know. But even for this very brief moment, there was not a thought of this stranger's fate. All this killer thought about, was his freedom in a world full of hate. Here where judgment was often given, a breech seemed to be in their law. A killer was free and the innocent condemned, taking the place for all. The Savior would take the place of the guilty, for no cost could save their soul. He would lay His life down willingly, and pay their price in full. But what about the guilty ones, who would simply walk away? They never stop to thank the One, for saving them that day. Still the innocent one would die, as the guilty would seem to prevail. God would see His Son being crucified, for this plan just could not fail. So they asked freedom for the guilty, and hollered crucify to their King. They chose the law and refused the justice, and gave up everything. The law demanded justice for the guilty, and freedom to the innocent one. But on a cross, the guilty were set free, as justice met the Son. Every sin in the entire world would come to Calvary's hill. So that when the law demanded payment, Jesus stamped paid in full upon the bill.

The Child Live's

It is God who places the miracle of life, inside of the mother's womb. This is a person who will grow someday, and will brighten someone's room. Growing in this tiny space, while each cell is being multiplied. Will one day bring joy into the world, and see his mother outside. Everyday this child depends on another, who will always do what is right. To always take care of their body, and keep them safe each night. These tiny fingers are always moving, and are taking in each tone. Here they feel so safe and sound, for they are never left alone. But then a rumble then a noise, and a feeling like they have never felt before. This tiny life is being put to death, sent straight to heavens shore. What has happened to this special blessing and where will this child be. With another choice, another life that this world will never see. Tiny fingers wiggle, but nowhere on earth to be found. For someone made a solemn choice, before this baby made a sound. They reasoned this child was not living; it was someone they could not see. Yet so very many years ago, that child was you and me. Now you may have a right to make a choice, it is your body this is true. But the moment you entered into a relationship, a tiny person entered you. It did not ask to be put there, and it took so little space. Yet you never gave this child a choice, to enter the human race. Now you may not think that this baby was a blessing, it was just something that you had to do. But you can be thankful for one very special blessing, that your mother did not choose herself over you.

EYES WITH NO SIGHT

He came upon a man who was crying, and He wondered what it could be. The man told him I am blind in my eyes, all I want is my sight to see. The stranger said I have noticed your hands and your two legs that can carry you around. Some people cannot even reach out for a hug, and they have mouths that cannot utter a sound. Some men have sight that is perfect, and still they do not see. They are blind to the hurting and the poor; they pass them and let them be. The ones, who have legs can go into the world, yet cannot seem to get past their door. They are able to go out and help others, but just set home wishing for more. Now you have a brain to think pleasant thoughts, ones that will bring you pure delight. But you would rather set here complaining to others, about your terrible loss of sight. There are some who struggle to take a step or two, and some have no legs at all. Still they do not set here crying, they get up each time they fall. You must not be sad because your eyes do not see, and do not cry because you feel this loss. For long ago, I was battered and bruised, as I hung upon a cross. But I knew that day would soon be over, and the victory would be so sweet. For every soul who were once feeling broken, could now become complete. You see eyes do not make you see any better, and a mouth has no power to feel. Yet all who place their lives in God's hands will find their faith is real. So call on the One who can give you your sight, His salvation is always free. Then the next time you are crying, because you are blind to the truth, ask the Lord and he will help you to see.

Someday We Will Meet Again

My parents have both departed this life, and the pain I try to hide. I know they are both in heaven, and still it hurts inside. So many times, I think about those things that I forgot to say. Now I know that our lives are here but a moment, and could quickly pass away. I remembered how our life was, with the many times we felt pain. Yet none of us were Christians, so our labor was in vain. My dad was first to leave this life and my mother barely cried. I thought she did not love him, because she kept her pain inside. But after my mother passed away, her letters broke my heart. She spoke about how much she missed him, how her life was torn apart. Oh if only I could see her again, and explain just how I feel. Yet they have died and gone to heaven; still the pain is so unreal. I know they are in a better place, where they will not be troubled with sin. Someday when I leave this life, we will surely meet again. I tried to be a good son, and honor my mom and dad. But I was not always there for them, and the pain I feel is bad. My Father please take care of them, they are in Your loving hand. I wish that they were here with me, but I will try to understand. They will never know the heartache, or the pain that they once knew. I know they are better then they have ever been, because now they are in heaven with You. I really miss my mom and dad, two people whose memory I love. Someday we will meet again, in our heavenly home above.

You Are My Lord

Jesus we say we know You, then our faith begins to swerve. We have used Your grace as leverage, to get things we do not deserve. When we get around other believers that is when we make a show. Yet some believers are like secret Christians, this world will never know. They say that they believe in You, yet live as if You are not there. Though they know that they are hurting You, they act as if they do not care. Some are always in church every week, and never miss Your word. But in their daily living, it is as though they never heard. They have this form of Godliness, yet they do not have a clue. It is not how the world should see us; they should all be drawn to You. Yet Lord sometimes I feel I have not served You, because of all the people that I forgot to tell. I could be one voice in a dark place, maybe save a soul from hell. My Lord please forgive me for not telling them the truth, and for every victory that I have lost. Help me to remember Your sacrifice, and the awesome price it cost. Let me see Your precious blood, as it washes away our sin. Help me to tell a person about hell, before it's to late and they are thrown in. Then remind me of the reason, that You came to die for me. Then help me to shine in a dark place, so that this entire world will see. Let Your name be on my lips, each morning noon and night. So when that enemy starts his attack, I will always be ready to fight. Keep me on the right path, brandishing Your powerful sword. So the entire world will see You in me, because You are my wonderful Lord.

Not Glorified Yet

Some people say they do not believe in healing, and that it is no longer for today. But when they get sick and cannot find a cure, they ask for healing when they pray. They say there are no miracles, yet they pray for one to arrive. It really is a miracle, that these doubters are still alive. They say that God's salvation requires there be works to pay. But if you have to earn your salvation, then the gift is taken away. Then they say that if you are a Christian, you must never commit another sin. Yet God says if you confess to Him, He will forgive you once again. Now these saints have the right idea, that we all must be holy someday. Your body was not redeemed when you were saved, and your flesh remained that way. So when you tell others that they are evil, and act like you are God's chosen one. You will one day be disappointed, when you finally meet His Son. Jesus our Lord is Holy; let us make that crystal clear. He was holy before this world was made, and He was holy when He was here. Though His precious blood redeems us, our body is still of this earth. When He calls us all to heaven, we will complete our second birth. The day when you asked Him to save you, your spirit and soul were saved. Yet some think they are free from temptation, their mind is captured and enslaved. You do not have your glorified body, and there still is no good in you. But when your body is raised and changed, that is when you will be perfect too. Healing power was given for a reason, because your body is wearing out. Only God can heal your brokenness, if you will live by faith not doubt. Many miracles are everywhere, just open your eyes, and see. I used to be lost and now I am saved, and my Jesus lives in me.

LOVE YOUR MOTHER

While He was hanging on the cross that day, having finished His work at last. All of His suffering and all of His pain, would soon be in the past. Yet there was one more thing that He had to do, before His work was done. With the final moments before all was finished, by committing His mother to another son. He placed His mother into His closest friend's care, so she would be sheltered from all of harms way. Knowing that soon He would be raised from the grave, to see her another day. But seeing His mothers broken heart, brought tears as He spoke for her care. Hanging on the cross fulfilling salvation, the reason that He was there. He knew she was hurting and knew how she felt, but His dieing would have to be done. For the offering of God's holy sacrifice, would be given to save everyone. Here Mary's Lamb would save the world, and keep them from going to hell. She knew that this day would one day come, to see the death of Emmanuel. The God, who came to dwell with man, would now return to His throne. So John took Mary as his mother, so she would never be left alone. The story seemed like a short goodbye, with a mother's broken heart. Yet for this reason, He had come, and she knew they would have to part. Then as He placed her into His dear friends hands, His end now satisfied. He looked back up to His Father, lowered His head and the Savior died. Now even though this story is sad, it still has a glorious spin. For as they placed Him in a tomb, three days later He came back again.

The Path To Salvation

Who could walk the path He walked, being righteous and totally free. He stood there humble as they spit in His face, with His mind on you and me. With every fist that slammed into His face, they tore His beard apart. Yet He would endure this horrible torture, because we were all in His heart. They beat Him with their torturous whip; just try to imagine how that would feel. With every stripe laid on His back, each one was done to heal. Then they took thorns and weaved them together, to form a makeshift crown. Then on His head, they placed it, and then they forced it down. Then as He stood there bleeding, He was beaten, tired and cold. He knew He would soon be put to death, but until then He would have to hold. They placed a crossbeam on His back, and each movement caused flesh to tear. Yet until He hung upon that cross, this pain He would have to bare. As He reached the place they called the skull, they threw Him to the ground. They drove the nails into His hands and feet, yet His mercy would abound. There in pain and agony with His thoughts on this world too. He cried Father please forgive them; they know not what they do. Then His moment had finally arrived, as He hung there on that cross. The world that was lost would soon be redeemed, and hell would feel the loss. Even the thief beside Him, would see His loving grace. When he asked the Lord's forgiveness, in that cold and cruel place. The devil felt the shock set in, by this plan he could not see. When three days were past and Jesus left hell, and set the captives free. The end is still not over, but the end of evil is near. For Jesus said He is coming back, and one day He will be here.

Provoke Not Your Children

Parents provoke not your children to wrath, for the way that they behave. For you cannot throw all the blame on them, for the example that you gave. When you tell your child not to swear, and they listen to what you say. If they have heard you speaking filthy words, they think that it is ok. Then when you tell them not to smoke, but you light up one for the road. When others convince them to try it out, they will do what they are told. For children copy the pattern that they see their parents do. So when you want them to do what is right, then it has to start with you. A child has to be punished, when you know that they have done wrong. You also have to praise them, to show them they belong. Do not give your children to the devil, but protect them day and night. Don't let them do what you know is wrong, but be an example to what is right. They can surely be a blessing, but not if you let them roam. It is up to you to bring them to God, so practice your faith at home. If you have let them do just as they please, that habit must be broke. Yet to stop your child's rebellion, give them love do not provoke. Go to God in prayer for them, and place your children in His care. You cannot do it by yourself you will not get anywhere. God will start to guide you, and He will show you what to do. But the way you raise your children my friend, is completely up to you.

CHILDREN OBEY YOUR PARENT'S

Children obey your parent's, for this is the way that it should be. Sometimes this may seem difficult, but God will help you to see. Think back to when you were a baby, too young to even know. Your parents could have given you up, but instead they helped you grow. Some kids have only one parent, and then there are others that have none. Little tears that cry for love, being alone is never fun. Remember when you were sick as a child, and needed a helping hand. You cried out to the one who loved you, and knew they would understand. Well most of us are bound to be hurt, by the ones we love so dear. But think of how you will feel, when your parents are no longer here. God knew we needed help in this life, and our parents would not always be right. But tell me now what you would do, if your parents were nowhere in sight. Would you be ready for what would lie ahead, just to grow up on your own? Would you be feeling empty inside, when you realize you are all alone? Right now, you may have the answers, that to you just may seem right. Yet what if you were to stand before God, would you know what to say tonight? You may not like His judgment, but your words will not mean a thing. Because God is the One who said you must obey, and He is Lord and King. So as you take your time to think, of what your parents should do. Just think of the way you are treating them, your problem just may be you. If you really want to be happy, with joy that will last day and night. Just obey your parents in the Lord, my children this is right.

Don't Be Late

As I left that place in a hurry, those words burning in my mind. If you leave this life tonight without Jesus, you will not like what you may find. Who gave him the right, to speak like that? He is just paranoid and telling lies. Yet I wish I would have listened to him, for this night brought a different surprise. I was driving home and angry, and my mind was filled with hate. I never saw the drunken driver, and my reaction was too late. All the lights began to fade, as darkness enveloped my soul. I felt like my spirit was being ripped from my body, and dragged down I fiery hole. Then pain began to engulf me, like a flame that would not die. Then my mind snapped back to that preacher, and I knew that he did not lie. Here I was in this horrible place, and there was nothing that I could do. So in an uncontrollable burst of pain, I screamed Jesus I need You. But there I stood in silent darkness; I was suffering as I met my fate. If only I could have one more chance, but now it was too late. I would gladly kneel before the Lord, and tell Him Jesus You are the King. Yet I knew that was impossible, I was in eternity feeling deaths sting. Oh why did I doubt what that preacher said, why did I think I was so cleaver? Now I was lost forever in hell, to suffer in here forever. I raised my voice with all I had and in this pain; I could hear my self scream. Then in this horrible moment I was shaken awake, and praise the Lord, it was only a dream. I fell on my face and asked Jesus to save me, so that I would never return to that place. He heard my voice and filled my heart, with His wonderful loving grace.

THE BIBLE

The bible is God's word to all, a most intelligent plan. He chose the easiest way He could, that would help us too understand. Yet we must keep in mind that His ways are higher, He is God, and we are man. He made a person into flesh and blood, with nothing more then sand. The bible is made with many books, and each one had something too say. He placed them there to give us knowledge, and to show us all the way. It is more then just a road map and many have studied this book. You may see only religious writing, but stop and take a closer look. Listen to what God is saying, and make sure that His message is clear. You just may find He is speaking to you, with a message for you to hear. Sometimes He speaks in a spiritual story, and you can find what is hidden there. He may be telling you what heaven is like, just keep searching if you dare. The pages point from beginning to end, and from the future to the past. Yet His message will always bring new hope, with faith that will always last. With many tribes and wars that are waged, and kings that will stand or fall. But in His word, you discover the Lord, for He is in it all. Do you see Him next to Samson, as those pillars start too crumble? Or can you see Him speaking to the human Job, as his friends all learn to be humble? Can you see Him hanging on the cross, with compassion in His eyes? Just read His book it is full of love, from a God who never lies. All He tells us is what He wants us to know, and yet there are some who will never see. The bible is there for all to read, yet some just let it be. But one day soon God is coming again, and then the world will know His word is true. All those who know what is written there, will know what they must do. There is a message of salvation, and the gift that is given free. It will save the sinner and change the doubter, just wait and you will see. For God loved us so very much, that He gave His only

Son. The fate of this world was in His hands and in Jesus His word was done. Everything God wanted to say, and every message that would be heard. Came to earth to save us all, Jesus is that word.

Never Grow Weary

When a person first becomes a Christian, their faith is such a delight. Yet over the years as they face many trials, they grow weary and lose some of their light. At first, they start out like a little child, relying on their Father's care. They trust what He says and then they act on it, knowing He is always there. Yet when the cares of this life get to heavy and their burdens get to hard to bare. They turn their faith into worry, and stop trusting in their Father's care. Well if you want to grow in your Christian walk, you must be ready to go out on a limb. You must walk by faith and not by sight, completely trusting in Him. Faith is not setting down on a chair, and believing it will always be. It is putting your trust in whatever God say's, by believing the things you cannot see. Many trials will come and go, but you can conquer every one. Yet you will have to place your trust in God, by believing in His Son. Even Peter walked on the water, though he was distracted, at least he tried. When he asked the Lord for the faith to come, his request was not denied. God has given us many gifts, to be used in marvelous ways. If we use these gifts to serve the Lord, our faith in His promise stays. You have to keep your faith burning bright, even though it seems like you may lose. Just go wherever He sends you, and be ready for Him to choose. Let the fire of the Holy Spirit; be inside you day and night. That the world may see you are a Christian, and will be drawn to God's holy light. Then one day if you start to grow weary, just remember what you should do. Ask the Lord to give you the power, for He lives inside of you. Never put your hand to the plow, unless His work you intend to complete. Then the Lord will give you a special crown, to one day lay down at His feet.

Jesus Is His Name

He is my anchor in the deepest sea, the calm before the storm. The Potter who will mold and shape me, to see what He will form. The Healer of the broken hearted, who opens blinded eyes. The One who removes their bondage, to reveals the devils lies. He is the Carpenter from Nazareth, who builds eternal homes. Up above in a place called heaven, where evil never roams. He is my peace when I am in trouble, and the Lifter of my head. The promise of eternal life, the resurrection from the dead. He is my hope in times of hopelessness, and my faith so I can believe. He is the gift from the Father above; He is the blessing I receive. He is the One who hung on the cross, who removed my guilt and shame. The One who has the name of Jesus, with power in His name. He loved me before I became a Christian, and is with me every day. His precious Holy Spirit is one who teaches me to pray. The bible tells about Him, He is the One who is called the Word. He is the Still Small Voice inside of me, just waiting to be heard. In fellowship, He is always there, and He never misses a day. He will never leave or forsake me, but will go with me all the way. What a special friend I have in Jesus and no other friend will do. He sticks closer then a brother and with His life, He saved us too. My all in all no matter what, the Shepard of my soul. He came to live inside of me, and promised He would never go. Do you want to have Him as your friend? I will show you where to start. Just tell Him that you need Him, and invite Him into your heart. Then you will find a perfect peace, and your life will never be the same. For only one has the power to save you, and Jesus is His name.

Born Twice

I was born in nineteen fifty six, and born again in eighty five. The first time I was born into death, and the second time made alive. The first time my soul was empty, but the second time God came in. So now, the first rejoices every day to leave behind the sin. Many times, I carried the weight of the sins I chose to bare. But the day my old life was put to death, the burden was no longer there. Now I have this new life, where I will never die again. For Jesus gave me a better life, completely free of sin. Two times, I was born yet I have died only once, for that old me was crucified. No more will I live to please myself, or the sin that I wished I could hide. I am filled with the love of the Father, with Jesus living in my heart. It is time for me to live for Him, for He has already done His part. The first time I was born into a curse, where sin was in control. I was heading for certain disaster and would have surely lost my soul. But on the day when I met the Lord, I found His truth could set me free. So I asked the Lord to save my soul, so He came to live in me. I am born again, washed in His blood, and I will never have to die. For He promised me eternal life, and my Savior does not lie. I am saved by grace and filled with His Spirit, and will forever be alive. Though I was born in nineteen fifty six, my real birth was in eighty five. The day I gave my life to Jesus, by calling on His name. That old man died and I was born again, and I will never again be the same.

He First Loved Me

I love to sing and write about Jesus, and all of the things that He did. To read the many parables, and all the wisdom He once said. I love to see when a person is saved, when they come to know God's Son. I love to feel secure in the Lord, as each new day is finally done. I love to see when someone is healed, just knowing Who preformed this deed. I love to give where He tells me to, because He always blesses the seed. I love to think about how I first got saved, where would I have been without Him? I love to watch people grow in their faith; they just jump into the water and swim. I love to see the multitudes gather, to see His works being done. I love to hear the word of the Father, saying listen to my Son. I love to think of heaven, and the many sights I will see. I love to think of Who is waiting there, ready to welcome me. I love the thought of seeing His throne, where Jesus is setting down. I love the thought of being there, just standing on holy ground. I love being in that place that is so awesome, where my Father will provide. I love being close to my precious Lord Jesus, just standing there by His side. I love everything about my Savior, and my heavenly family tree. But do you know why I love him with all of my heart; it is because He first loved me.

Who Is This Man

Who is this Man who speaks to the storm, and it quiets before our eyes? Who is this Teacher who knows what they are thinking, and reveals their wicked lies. Who is this Physician who can heal their sickness, where no doctor could before? He opens eyes and cast out devils, and heals the multitudes by the shore. Who is this Leader who can walk on water, and can make food to feed them all? Who is this Man who chooses few, to follow His chosen call? Who is this Preacher who can baptize with fire, and who causes their hearts to melt? Who is this Rabbi who speaks God's word, with great power that is felt? Where did He come from does anyone know, and tell me why is He on that cross? We could have learned who He truly was, oh what a terrible loss. But look again He is not finished; He has risen from the dead. Now I know He is my Savior, who took my punishment instead. Only God could do all He has done, to remove all my guilt and shame. Does any one know just who He is, who never cast the blame. Please tell how you came to know Him, so that I may do the same. Now I know, He is the Son of God, and Jesus is His name.

The Time Of Jacob's Trouble

The tribulation will be a time of trouble, like never on earth before. Now you may believe it is the time you will be tested, you have no idea what is in store. A time when the restraining hand of goodness, has been fully taken away. This planet will be filled with every kind of evil, and no one will want to stay. There will not be any talk of abortion, for murder will be commonplace. The devil will go on a violent rage, to destroy the human race. There will be killing without the justice, and hatred with out a cause. All who go through this terrible time, will feel that dragons claws. Those who venture to take his mark or the number of his name. Will forfeit their eternal soul forever, and receive his punishment the same. Strong delusion will come to all, and it will be hard to make a choice. When you call out to the One who can help, He just may not hear your voice. Parents will then betray their children, even unto death. They will not care if they are safe or in trouble, they will have evil on their breath. The love of many will grow cold, and life will lose its cost. Those who take the mark of the beast will become eternally lost. Do you think that you will survive in this world, where nothing is ever right? Where darkness has blinded everyone's eyes, and kept them away from the light. This is the time; God will pour out His wrath, on the devil and on sinful man. For all the evil done on planet earth and for every ones wicked plan. This time is called Jacob's trouble, and will force man to fall to their knees. Every person will see the truth, as the power of darkness flees. Many will lose their heads in this time, and many will give up their souls. But God has warned you ahead of time, of this day that the devil knows. Do not set there waiting for the time of trouble, it is time to call on God's Son. That devil may think he can win this war, but the battle is already won.

False Fame

The children today are caught in a trap, of all the glitter of the Hollywood stars. The music has taken control of their thoughts, like a prisoner behind steel bars. The pressure they face has been magnified, by their friends, and their own disgrace. All that they have will be taken away, and another will steal their place. Their fame has reached the pinnacle of success, like an idol that is starting to grow. They are walking a road that every one is walking, yet they never can reach their goal. Many will be confused as the end draws near, for who can protect their today? They have lost all the time they were given, and now they have nothing to say. God is preparing to stop all this madness, and come and take His rightful place. Every soul rather good or bad will stand and see His face. No movie star or famous singer will have a good defense. For the rap, the pop, and the rock and roll will never again make sense. Now you may have been the most popular person that every one wanted to see. But when the Lord calls you to stand before Him, your beauty will just not be. You can joke or laugh, and make fun if you wish, and even say this is not true. But what will you say to the living God, who is staring back at you? All your songs will not mean a thing, and you can flaunt your beauty galore. But no one will end your judgment day, where your beauty will be no more. You can win the American idol on earth, and this world may think you are great. But when you stand before the God of all, repenting will be too late. Walk with the crowd and do what they do, and even cling to every fad. But remember God will someday judge you, and remove all the things you once had. Just look at what this world is like today, how much longer do you think this will last. Now you can call Him to save your soul, but soon even this time will pass. Get your mind out of that prison; and tell that devil you have had enough. Do not fall for his tricks anymore, for soon, it is going to get rough. Those famous crowds are walking a road to destruction, with an end that is soon to be. For God is getting ready to judge us all, and this truth you are about to see. Call on God to save your soul, for you may only have today, do not continue to press your luck, or there may be hell to pay.

Why I Preach

The reason why I preach so much let me see if I can explain. Just turn your television on tonight, and you will see a world gone insane. Like the ones who gamble all their money, then complain that they are broke. Some folks set around choking, just because they like to smoke. Some are getting diseases that just may end their life. Because they were just not satisfied, staying with their husband or their wife. Then you have the ones taking drugs, searching for that mega high. Yet all it takes is too much mega, and these people can say goodbye. How about those who set in bars, just sucking down kegs of beer. Then they try to drive themselves home, way to drunk to even steer. With all the things they are doing that is crazy, one thing I am sure is true. The world is heading down a darkened road, and what will become of you? All the things that are happening today will soon be too hard to bare. The day is soon approaching, that will show you did not care. Then His book will open, but your name will not be seen. You could have heard the preaching, but you lingered in between. He will turn to you in judgment, and the end will come at last. The entire world will hear the truth, as He finally reads your past. No matter what you say to Him, forgiveness will not be. The day you thought would never come, has arrived for all to see. You said the gift He offered, you would think about someday. Yet now as you stand before Him, that gift was taken away. So you ask me why I preach so much, well I guess it is time to tell. It is so you can know the Savior, and escape the flames of hell. This is the reason why I preach, for Jesus died to save your soul. He wants me to tell you that He loves you, and He wants to make you whole. I preach because there is not much time, and I am hoping that you will see. That the greatest preacher there has ever been is living inside of me.

In Me

In sickness, He is my Healer, in poverty He is my Supply. In weakness, He is my Strength and Shield, and in need my El Shaddai. In trouble, He is my High Tower, in shame the Lifter of my head. In thirst my River that flows within, in hunger the Broken Bread. In doubt, He is the Faith I need, and in faith, the All Knowing One. In life, He is the Breath in me, and in truth God's only Son. In glory, He is the King of Kings, in salvation the Lamb that was slain. In want, He is my All in All; in hurt, He removes my pain. In blessings the Giver of all good gifts and in loss He is the miracle I need. In freedom, He is my Deliverer, and in the harvest, He is all my seed. In heaven, He is the Lord of Lord's, and on His throne, He is the Judge. In death, He is the Comforter, and in the law, He will not budge. In wisdom He is the source of all knowledge; in my burden He carries my load. In the bible, He is the Redeemer, the greatest story that has ever been told. In sadness He is the Joy that fills, when I am alone He is the Friend who is there. When I am wondering if He loves me, that's when He gives me His tender care. Here on earth He is my Helper, who is sent to me from above. In me, He is my Jesus, who is the One I truly love. Who is He to you my friend, have you even stopped to see? Jesus is the one I am talking about, who is Everything to me.

THE PRICE

What will really get us in to heaven, is it the good things we all do?
Like lending money to someone in need, who just may ask of you. What
about giving your things away, maybe things you have finally out grew.
Does that puff your pride to that higher level, as they take that gift from
you? Will this be enough to get you into heaven, where no sin will ever
be found? Are you really sure, you will make it there are you sure, you
are heaven bound? What about your giving, the tithes and offerings and
such. Is that enough to grant you entrance, are you sure you have not
given too much. Are you the friendly usher or the greeter all the time?
Is there any that can take your place, is this something you would not
mind? Well none of the things that were mentioned, can get you into
that place. For nothing, we do will be good enough, to permit us to see
His face. God has made the only way; and there is no other one. You
have to believe in Jesus, salvation is in His Son. Doing deeds will never
save you, and your giving is still the same. For Jesus is the Only Way,
you must call upon His name. It will not matter who you are or who
you claim to be. Jesus is the Savior who can save and set you free. So if
your faith is in someone else, and you have heaven in your sight. You
had better call on Jesus, for your life could be over tonight. So do not
put your trust in your good works, for the price you cannot pay. If you
try to get to heaven without Jesus, your salvation will be taken away.

Thy Will Be Done

Oh, cover me over my Father above, with the blood that can cleanse and make free. See if inside I have any hidden sin, for You know what is inside of me. Please take all my anger and hate, and change every evil way I know. Help me to live like Your little child wash and make me whiter then snow. Place within me love, peace, and joy, and help me to love everyone. Then help me to live the way You want me too, and then let Your will be done. Father please make me like Jesus, with a heart of a servant inside. Teach me to walk in the paths where You lead me, Holy Spirit please come and be my guide. If I should face the enemy, and not know what I should do. Help me to stand on Your word my Lord, help me to trust in You. Take every thought that is not from You, and wash them from my mind. For I give You all authority my Lord, to remove every evil you find. I truly wish to be holy my Lord, but temptation is all around. Yet I want to live in that wonderful place, where no evil will ever be found. I wait upon You Lord with all of my heart, for the day when You will come back again. So that I can live with You my Lord, completely free of all sin. Help me to live like Your wonderful Son Jesus, teach me to walk in Your love. Then let Your will be done on this earth Lord, as it is in heaven above.

Praise Jesus It Won't Be Long

My children I wonder how long it will be, before this old life is finally through. Many years ago when I was young, I helped you along as you grew. I was there each time you were hurting, even when I was all alone. Though the years have been really hard on me, the scars of my pain are not shown. My door was often open, when you needed a place to stay. I fed and even cared for you, and I helped you along the way. There have been times I have had my bad days, but I loved you still the same. I always made sure there was coffee on the table, almost every time you came. Now that I have grown older, I set here wondering if you still care. I am growing weary and getting tired all the time. I may need help, but will you be there? I know I may be difficult, and your patience may grow thin. Yet what if I have no place to go, my child will you take me in? Every day I set here waiting for my Lord to come and set me free. I wait for Him to call me to heaven, so that no one will be burdened with me. I only hope that you remember just how much I really care. For one day, you may look for me, but I will not be there. So please cherish this time that we now have, and forgive me if I have done wrong. Soon I may be going home, praise Jesus it will not be long.

My Quiet Place

I come to you my Jesus, in the quiet of my heart. Where I am free from the cares of this life, and the troubles that sometimes start. I know that I have not spent much time with You Lord, there in our quiet place. Where I listen to Your precious Spirit, as I seek Your holy face. Please forgive me for this sin my Lord, for not knowing what I should do. I could have avoided the cares of this life, if I would have kept my eyes on You. I know that worrying about the trouble in this life, will never ease the pain. It is like rubbing oil on our sins, trying to remove the stain. But I am concerned about only one thing; it is something I desire to do. To come to a place where nothing means more, then spending my time with You. I love You Jesus with all of my being, and all that I would like to see. Is a quiet place where I can sup with You Lord, and where You can talk with me. Where I will hear the things You speak, and obey Your every word. Where that still small voice inside of me, will every time be heard. A quiet place where I am praying alone and the world is left at the door. Where You and I are fellowshipping, the way we did before. My wonderful Savior I love You, and I want to just feel Your love, and one day set and fellowship, in Your kingdom up above. Until I am there with You my Lord, please show me where to start. Then meet me in my quiet place, which is found inside my heart.

RUNNING FROM SALVATION

One day I realized I was empty inside, and I felt so all alone. I tried to fill the void within, with the things, which I had sown. But as I searched for my answer, a voice called out my name. I was afraid of the One who called out to me, for I was aware of all my shame. I ran out the door and hurried away, trying to flee this light. Yet the ground opened up in front of me, and I quickly fell from sight. I felt like I was falling into a deep cavern, where the darkness was very thick. With the smell of fire and sulfur, and an odor that made you sick. Then I heard that voice again, but I was ready to listen instead. I wondered if I could be dreaming, or maybe I was dead. But then I saw a hand reach down I saw His scars and I thought I was done. I had Tears in my eyes as He spoke and said; I am Jesus the Savior God's Son. He pulled me up to safety, as I lay there on the ground. I knew that I was lost without Him, but now, I had been found. He came and knelt down beside me, and with tears, I saw Him grieve. He said I have called to you many times, but you would always turn and leave. I could not understand why He cared for me, so I hung my head in shame. This Person knows I am a sinner, and loves me still the same. He placed His hand on my shoulder, and said it will be ok. I promise I will never leave you; just believe Me and I will stay. I said but Lord I am a sinner, and I do not deserve to live. He smiled and said I know that, but My grace I came to give. I said then what can I give to repay You, for dieing in my place. Only believe and put your faith in Me, and receive My gift of grace. The reason why I called to you was, you were crying in your heart. You felt alone without any hope, and did not know where to start. So I called your name so many times, so that you would know the way. Now the choice is placed back in your hands, and it is up to you today. Now is your day of salvation, you can no longer run and hide. You can live forever in heaven, but it is up to you to decide.

NEW BORN KING

There were three wise men that followed a star, from faraway lands they came. For they had heard of God's great salvation, to be sent to bare His name. They wandered through the wastelands and deserts, in search for this promised king. They were hoping to see and to deliver in person, all the treasure that they would bring. They arrived in front of a meager inn, and they saw the stall where the star had shown down. They walked around and entered the stall, and stood in awe at what they found. There in a lowly manger, lay the Savior of all the earth. They laid their gifts before Him, the best of all their worth. Here they knelt before the God of the universe, so frail and yet so alive. They now saw that God had kept His word, that one day He would arrive. Wise men and Shepard's and even angels, worshiped and rejoiced that night. For all the world that were walking in darkness, received this wonderful light. Mary and Joseph just stood in awe, as they beheld their newborn Son. A vision that would forever be burned into their hearts, seeing them worship this Holy One. Then everyone heard a heavenly host, say, unto you is born this day. Here in the city of David, One who will wash all your sins away. They said peace on earth good will to men let all creation now sing. For unto you He is born today, Jesus Christ the Newborn King.

RICHES AND FAME

If I were to gain both riches and fame, and this whole world laid out for my use. How would I act in this foolish dream, in the end what would be my excuse? Would I say it was mine, to do as I please or would I simply not enter my plea? If I gained everything I could ever imagine, I wonder what would happen to me. Is my life worth more to me then riches; is my health more valuable then fame? Was this world created for only me, with the deed imprinted with my name? The answer to these questions many souls have sought out, and have wondered about for so long. Yet every time they have searched for the truth, they discovered their answers were wrong. You see riches can buy only temporal things that someday will pass away. Your fame will last for only so long, but the glory will never stay. The world we live in will come to its end, and your riches will be no more. For only God has the answer, to what this world was created for. With Him, there is no need for money, and a servant is more prized then fame. This world's wisdom is hardly worth a thought, but to serve the Lord is always great gain. What good would it do for you to gain this whole world, and one day forfeit your soul? Where would you find those things that you craved, and where is the place you will go. Those who have placed God above everything else have laid it all down in His name. They know all the wealth belongs to the Lord, and to Him belongs all the fame. One day soon, we will see His face, in a place more precious then riches untold. We will be with Jesus in heaven above, walking on those streets of gold.

THE MARTYR'S HOPE

Long ago, many Christians were tortured; they had faith that just would not fail. Many of them had family they loved, who were made slaves or thrown in jail. These saints were told to deny their faith, to escape before it was too late. They were sealed by the Son of God; and were ready to accept their fate. Some were hung on poles and burned, while others witnessed before they died. Still others were fed to hungry lions, and many were crucified. These Christians stood at the doorway to death, and yet they refused to deny their Lord. They were even thrown into dungeons, to feel the cold steel of the sword. Every one of them, who were put to death, would cause the word to grow. Put to death for what they believed, so that their God all this world would know. They even place them on racks that would stretch them, causing their limbs to part. Others watched as their families suffered, which only broke their heart. Still they would not give up their salvation; their faith meant more then their life. Many of them suffered horrible deaths, while many were put to the knife. Every evil under the sun, to stop them from preaching the word. But every time persecution came, the message of salvation was heard. Jesus said you will have tribulation, and they tortured the Master too. He was mocked, beaten, and put to death, and they will do the same to you. Now you may not have been called to lay down your life, for the faith in which you believe. But one day you may face that moment, where death you could receive. You will not have to go it alone, and there will be no place that you can hide. Jesus will keep you faithful; He will be standing by your side. Just keep the faith no matter what happens, and remember the reason why. Christians may be put to death, but our God we will never deny.

THE CHOICE

In the Garden of Eden many years ago, life was always good. Adam and Eve fellowshipped with God, just as He knew they would. Eve was the first to taste the forbidden fruit; she knew this was not right. She did not want to go it alone, so she told Adam to take a bite. Many years have gone by since that day, with children born to the human race. Man still joins in this rebellion, for he had lost his chosen place. The devil stripped him of the right, to receive the blessings like before. The choice he once had was taken away; he had the freedom to choose no more. Day and night, over, and over, it all remained the same. It was all because he joined in the sin, and doubled up the blame. God was always merciful, always ready to forgive. His way required redemption, which would show men how to live. Man became used to his wicked ways, and ready to except his loss. Yet God had another plan in mind, which would point them too the cross. No one was worthy to bring redemption, the salvation that would save every man. It would require a perfect sacrifice, and this only God could command. Jesus allowed Himself to be put to death, and then rose up from the grave. So that by His death and resurrection, the world He now would save. Man still had the problem with obedience, but God's word became a voice. He would teach the man how to come back to God, and then give him back the choice.

Holy Ghost Fire

Do you want to do more for Jesus; are you ready to walk in His word? Do you want others to know you belong to Him; do you want you're preaching to be heard? Well this world is lost without Him, they will not believe until they are told. You have to want that person saved, so stand up, and then be bold. When Jesus started His walk to the cross, many believed along the way. No man ever spoke as He did; they listened to every word He would say. When He healed the sick, they would be healed, when He cast out a demon it would leave. Those who were oppressed by the devil, His deliverance they all would receive. Today we are afraid of what people will think, even though He lives in our heart. There is no special time we should start to witness; all we have to do is start. The Holy Spirit will give you the words, He will tell you what to say. However, you have to take authority, and tell that devil to go away. You are a child of the living God, ambassadors of the Lord. God gave you a powerful weapon, His word as a two edged sword. Take His word to a world that is lost, and lead them to His light. Then there will be rejoicing in heaven, as they come to Him this night. Do what Jesus asked you to do, be a witness in a darkened place. Show someone the love of the Father, and then tell them about His grace. Tell that devil to hit the road, and then fear will hit the street. For the only place that devil belongs, is underneath your feet. If you have always wanted to do something for Jesus and it has always been your desire. Grab your bible and open your mouth, and speak with Holy Ghost fire.

You Must Master It

A believer, who says they love the Lord, yet cannot get past their sin. Will walk around always feeling defeated, and lose their joy again. It is true the Father will forgive you, and have mercy if you will confess. He wants you to be more then conqueror's, because He made you the very best. Some have made this a form of escape, so they can sin another day. Yet God wants you to overcome, and to put those sins away. Jesus really love's you, and stands ready to forgive. He knows you could be an awesome Christian, if you just learn how to live. If you will ask the Lord to lead you, His Spirit will show the way. You can truly have a relationship with God and fellowship everyday. For everyone who continues to sin, will one day think it is ok. They will follow every evil on earth, as sin lures them away. If you do not turn from those wicked ways, then sin will never part. Then you will never repent to God, you will have a hardened heart. Let the Lord show you how to live, he will come and remove your sin. Then you will be filled with joy unspeakable, and fellowship will begin. Take those old familiar sins and confess them all today, then God will cover you in the blood of Jesus and wash them all away.

Lift Your Voice In Praise

Holy, Holy, Holy, unto our awesome God we sing. Worthy is the Savior, give praise to our Lord and King. Sing unto Him a new song, of honor and glory too. Then tell it from the housetops, that Jesus Christ loves you. Come bow down before the Lamb, and offer to Him your praise. Acknowledge Him in all you do, and honor Him in all your ways. Dance before the God of all, and let Him know you care. Lift your voice up to His throne, and show Him you are there. Praise our Lord both day and night, let His joy be in your mind. Worship Him now and forever, and praise Him all the time. Fear the Lord with all your heart, give praise to Him today. Let all your prayers go up before Him, as you kneel down to pray. Go before our Holy Father; raise your hands without any doubt. With all the joy, you can muster up, get excited, and let it out. Sing, and dance, and praise before Him, and make a joyful noise. Let Him see the real you, and just lose your perfect poise. Tell the Lord how much you love Him; come in Spirit and in truth today. Leason to what He is saying to you, worship Him in every way. Decide today to turn to Him, and make your life a living praise. Keep Him in your heart and mind; worship Him all of your days. Lift up your prayers as a sweet aroma that will come up before His face. Then receive His sweet anointing, as He pours out His loving grace. Remember His Spirit lives in you, and rejoice when each day is done. God will receive all of the glory and honor, from those who worship His Son.

The Word Of Your Testimony

What was the reason you came to the Lord, was it a voice which called your name? Were you at a point where nothing mattered, or was life to you a game? Well no one will come to God to be saved, unless they first are called. If they are asked to come before they are ready, the invitation may be stalled. God knows every person's state, and He knows who will accept His Son. Some will be saved in a moment, while others may never come. Every person has that choice, to except His gift of grace. Then they will become a witness, in a very special place. Your testimony is a book that is read, and just may open the eyes of the lost. The way you received eternal life, was free and without cost. By telling others how you came to believe, washed in the blood of God's Son. That testimony may speak to many, or ignite the soul of just one. By the blood of the Lamb, and the word of your testimony, you have learned to overcome. Telling the lost how you came to know Him, and where He has brought you from. There just may be someone who is in that place, where you once used to be. When they hear about how you were delivered, then they may want to get free. So always, remember you are a living testimony, of what God's love can do. When you were a sinner, and needed a Savior, Jesus came and died for you.

New Jerusalem

Glory like none seen before, with no need of the sun for light. Here in this city where the living God dwells, with no darkness and no night. This place where peace always fills the air, where love always flows so free. This is the place of lasting joy, where His glory will always be. This kind of life man has always searched for, where people could live as one. A place where everyone serves each other, where the ruler is God's Son. Having no more lack and no starving souls, no sickness, sin, or war. There will be no more killing anywhere, for death will be no more. Everyone will join the songs of praise, where no sadness will ever be found. For in this city the law will be righteous, and God's kingdom will always abound. The lion and the lamb will lie down together, with laughter on every child's face. No one will ever cause trouble again, for no problems can enter this place. There will be no more hatred, and no more anger, and all pain will have to go. God will supply every seed for your harvest, and His love will make it grow. This is a city that will have room for every person, with plenty of space for all. It will not matter what portion you choose, there is enough for the great and the small. The doors to this city will always be opened, yet no evil will ever get in. for this is a city that will always be holy, completely free of sin. Do you want to live in this wonderful kingdom, Then ask Jesus to save your soul. Then when this city comes down from heaven, then that is where you will go. Make the choice now before it is to late, for the place you would like to see. As for me and my house we have chosen the Lord, and in His kingdom is where we will be.

Is That Jesus You See

Whose image do you see when you look in your mirror? Take a closer look, and it may become clearer. Are you seeing the person that you claim to be, or seeing the person you want others to see. Your reflection is only the outside of you, but how do you know what the world will view? The outside of a person can be covered and changed. Disguised as a saint, and even rearranged. Yet the image in that mirror is what it was made to be. It may not show all, that we want others to see. But let us go to the inside, where we see what is true. That is where the entire world, will see the real you. If you are a smoker, you are destroying your lungs. If you are someone who swears, you are abusing your tongue. If you are a drinker, then you are not in your right mind. If you are taking drugs, it is no telling what you will find. The things we are doing may seem to be ok. Yet if you do not stop them now, they will never go away. Just stop for a moment, and see the person God created. He said it is good, but it is the sin that is hated. Our body is the temple, purchased on the cross. Yet if that temple is full of sin, tell me who feels the loss? Go back to your mirror; take a moment and just stare. Is this the real you, that you see standing there. Then think for one moment, how the world really sees's us. It is not you they are searching for, they are looking for Jesus.

Do You See

Do you see the spiritual battle, for the souls of mortal man? Do you see the shadow over them, the minds that do not understand? Do you see the hardness of their hearts, and the coldness of each touch? Do you see the world falling into darkness, where doing good is just too much? Do you know who is causing all of this evil; do you see him in their plight? Well then, take your eyes off that fallen angel, and look to God's great light. The spiritual battle for all of their souls is being won on every coast. Where people are saved and the enemy destroyed, as they encounter God's heavenly Host. Where the cross was placed so long ago, to mark redemptions flow. Where mortal man can come back to God and sin will have to go. Do you see the blood wash over them, and do you see them all made new? Do you see the grace come down from God, all the love He has for you? Do you see His Son hanging on that cross, to remove each darkened sin? Do you hear the promise from His lips that He will soon come back again? Do you know the angels are rejoicing, as your sins are washed away? Do you wait for Him to come again, could this be that wonderful day? Well do not worry about what you see, or what you may hear others say. A shout will sound from heaven, to catch us all away. Then we will see Him face to face, in His power and His might. So while you wait for His soon return, walk by faith and not by sight.

THE SAVIOR'S HEART

If you wish to see the Saviors heart, it starts in a lowly stable. Where you realize you are a sinner, come to Him if you are able. If you wish to see the Saviors heart, then follow Him to the cross. Where you crucify your old life, and let Jesus be your boss. If you wish to see the Saviors heart, then go to the empty tomb. Where you find that He is risen and no longer in that room. If you wish to see the Saviors heart, you must believe He is alive. Be ready when He calls to you, for His promise to arrive. If you wish to see the Saviors heart, come and kneel before His throne. Where you put your faith in no one else, but Jesus Christ alone. If you wish to see the Saviors heart, then lay your doubt aside. For He knows you needed a Savior, that is the reason why He died. So if you wish to see the Savior heart, then this is what you should do. Tell Him that you love and need Him, and He will come and live in you.

One Way

There is only one way you can get to heaven, and it does not matter what you think. The bible says you were created, not a part of some missing link. You will never get to God with your brilliance and might, and no religion can get you in. It is only by grace, which is the Lord's salvation that removes every person's sin. Now you may believe you are a good enough person, you have not robbed, cheated, or killed. Yet every person is born under a curse, and in sin we are over skilled. There is only one way to the Father, and Jesus said He is that Way. You can find it in the word of God, not only what you have heard me say. God said His Son paid our penalty, when He died upon that tree. To make atonement for every sin at that place they call Calvary. No other person was chosen to save us; it could only be God's Son. This is the way He planned from the beginning, and to God the decision is done. So you can choose which god you wish to serve, but getting to heaven requires one key. Jesus is the one who can get you to God, the only one there will ever be. By His birth, and His death, and resurrection, and His coming to receive His own. You will have to place your faith in Him, or pay for the sins you have sown. Jesus the Lord is the only way, the truth and the life there will be. So if you want to open the door to heaven, remember Jesus is that key.

Setting At His Table

They were seated at His table to eat this final meal. Some would speak of the miracles they witnessed, and the way it made them feel. While He spoke about His body, in the breaking of the bread. The wine to represent His blood, a remembrance once He was dead. Yet no one could see what He was seeing, the betrayal from within. They could not see the heart of the Savior, soon to die for every sin. They all loved to hear the mysteries, and the talk of His kingdom to come. Yet when He spoke of dieing on the cross, this was way too hard for some. They were setting here with the Son of God, singing hymns, and hearing Him speak. Here sat the Lion of the tribe of Judah, and the Lamb of God so meek. The hour of darkness was soon to arrive, where God's Son would choose to die. He would bring the world back to the Father, as they hollered crucify. All the sin past, present, and future, was now cast upon the Son. Jesus would pay for every soul, and God's will would now be done. There on a hill with a blood stained cross and new hope for every man. The God of the entire universe hung, fulfilling salvations plan. Yet this was not His finished work, for He rose up from the dead. So that everything written in His word would be done exactly as, He said. Now the world now brought down to its knees, with worship now made new. Where all could sit down at His table, and hear Him speaking too. To sing our hymns and know the mysteries, as we set in that heavenly place. At the table of the Lord and Savior, beholding Him face to face.

HE IS RISEN

On a beautiful sunny morning, as the earth was warm and bright. His followers were all still hidden away, from the tragedy the following night. No one had an inkling, of what had just taken place. All were busy trying to hide their fears, and cover their disgrace. Still this was a special morning, for a light was about to dawn. Yet these were in a state of shock, for their Master now was gone. They were thinking about the following week, would His promises now arrive? Then came a pounding at the door, open up the Master is alive. The woman stood there crying, telling all that they had heard. These who were in this place of mourning, were clinging to every word. Could this be true, they said to one another, let us go, and examine the tomb. But all they found were the grave cloths, but Jesus was not in the room. They hurried back behind locked doors, for fear of the enemy host. Then Jesus appeared before them, and they thought they had seen His ghost. He offered them to touch Him, now they knew He had risen from the dead. Just seeing Him standing there in the flesh, reminded them of the words He had said. The Son of God would be put to death, and three days later, rise again. He would bring to all salvation, and wash away their sin. Here they faced the God of all, in His flesh for them to see. When He comes again to take us home, that is how He will truly be. Jesus rose up from the dead, just the way He said He would do. One day soon, He will come again, and my friend we will see Him too.

Do You Still Have Doubt

There was a person long ago who believed that God was not real. He lived his life in unbelief, not caring how others would feel. That person did not want prayer in the schools, saying it was wrong to mix church and state. He also wanted to remove the pledge of allegiance, which he claimed was out of date. The Ten Commandments would have to go, because why should he worry about his sin? They should not be in any public places, for to him they did not fit in. All his threats came in evil lies, just pleading with his fiery breath. What was causing him to be so afraid, you mention God, and he was scared to death? Now he did not want to believe the gospel, or acknowledge that the bible was true. This would show him that he was a sinner, and had a need of a Savior too. Now it makes you wonder just who he calls on, when trouble comes his way. Does he call for any one or just remain silent, not knowing what to say. What will he think if he dies tonight and opens his eyes once more? Will he still have doubt and not believe the way he did before? I wonder what will happen, when he looks up to see God on His throne. Will he have anything there to say for himself, or will he feel so all alone. What if God looks down at him, and says do you believe in Me now. What will he do when he asks God to save him, and the answer he receives is how? Now you may not believe that God is real, and you may spend your life in doubt. Then God will send you into Hell, and will never let you out. That place was not prepared for you; a punishment no human should see. If you do not believe what He said is true, when you get there you will never be free. If you are one who will always doubt, and nothing can change your mind. If you die tonight, and see that God is real, you will not like what you find. You will not have a second chance to say that you were wrong. You will be thrown into the fires of hell and that place is where you will belong.

Conclusion:

In conclusion, I would just like to say; that before I had Jesus in my life I was forever searching for something to fill the void that I had in my heart. The day I invited Him into my heart, my whole life changed. When I placed my faith in His death and resurrection, I know He forgave my sins. He filled me with His Holy Spirit and I have never been the same, praise God. I am truly blest and you can be too. I now see things more differently, and He has blest me with a wonderful family. I have His assurance of eternal life, and you can have that too. Just invite Him into your heart, place your faith in Him and you will see the truth. That God is real and Jesus is one day coming back again. He is preparing a place for us right now, please call out to Him before it is too late. He loves you and will reach down from heaven, and touch you the same way He did me. Please do it today and May God give you the wisdom to act on His word. Receive your touch of heaven from our Savior's heart. God bless you, and I pray I will see you on the other side of eternity. In His, service forever, Gerald Bergeron.

Author Biography:

Gerald Bergeron has read and studied the bible for over twenty years. He was baptized in the Holy Spirit and was inspired to write Christian poetry. He lives in Grand Rapids Michigan, with his wife Betty, his three sons', Ernesto, Gerald, and James, and his daughter Ysidra.